Popular Complete Smart Series

Complete
FrenchSmart®

Grade
7

Contents

Vocabulaire : Les sports et les équipements

Révision : « Faire de... » et « jouer à... »

Grammaire : Les points cardinaux

Nous devons porter des casques pour faire du ski!

We must wear helmets when we ski!

A. Copiez les mots.

Copy the words.

à la montagne on the mountain

_____

ah lah mohn·tahny

faire de... to do...

le ski skiing

_____

luh skee

l'alpinisme mountain climbing

_____

lahl·pee·neezm

la luge sledding

_____

lah lewj

la planche à neige snowboarding

_____

la plaansh ah nehj

le casque
helmet

_____

luh kahsk

les bottes
boots

_____

leh boht

la planche à neige
snowboard

_____

la plaansh ah nehj

les skis
skis

_____

leh skee

les gants
gloves

_____

leh gaan

le télésiège
ski lift

_____

luh teh·leh·syehj

dans le ciel in the sky

daan luh syehl

à terre on land

ah tehr

faire de...
to do...

le parachutisme
parachuting

luh pah·rah·shew·teezm

le vol à voile
gliding

luh vohl ah vwahl

jouer à... to play...

le hockey
hockey

luh oh·keh

le soccer
soccer

luh soh·kehr

le tennis
tennis

luh teh·neess

le football américain
American football

luh foot·bohl ah·meh·ree·kahn

le base-ball
baseball

luh behz·bohl

le basket-ball
basketball

luh bahs·keht·bohl

à l'eau in water

ah loh

faire de... to do...

la natation
swimming

lah nah·tah·syohn

le canotage
canoeing

luh kah·noh·tahj

le canot
the canoe

luh kah·noh

la plongée sous-marine
scuba diving

lah plohn·jeh soo·mah·reen

la voile
sailing

lah vwahl

le gilet de sauvetage
life jacket

luh jee·leh duh sohv·tahj

le costume de bain
bathing suit

luh kohs·tewm duh bahn

1 Les sports – Sports

B. Remplissez les tirets.
Fill in the blanks.

A Quand il neige, j'aime aller à ___ ____t_g__ .

B Quand je fais d_ sk_ je prends le t__ési_g_ .

C Quand je fais du canotage je porte un g___t d_ s__vet_g_ .

D Je fais _u p_r_c__tis_e.

E Je joue _u soccer avec un b_ll_n de football.

C. Construisez des phrases avec les mots donnés. Imitez l'exemple.
Make sentences with the given words. Follow the example.

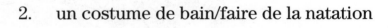

J'ai besoin d'un ballon de football pour jouer au soccer.

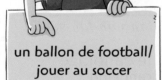

un ballon de football/ jouer au soccer

1. une raquette de tennis/jouer au tennis

   _____

2. un costume de bain/faire de la natation

   _____

3. un canot/faire du canotage

   _____

Complete FrenchSmart · Grade 7

Grammaire

If a sport is "played" in English, then use "jouer à" in French and if a sport is "not played", then you have to use "faire de" in French.

	la	l'	le
à	à la	à l'	au
de	de la	de l'	du

e.g.   Je joue au tennis.
       I play tennis.

       Je fais de la luge.
       I go sledding.

The verb "jouer" is conjugated like all regular "-ER" verbs of the first group, but "faire" is an irregular verb of the 3rd conjugation.

« faire »

je	fais
tu	fais
il/elle	fait
nous	faisons
vous	faites
ils/elles	font

D.   Complétez les phrases avec « faire de » ou « jouer à » selon le sport.
Complete the sentences with "faire de" or "jouer à" depending on the sport.

1.   Gilles, Olivier et Sarah (le ski) _____ en hiver.

2.   Jacques (l'alpinisme) _____ dans les montagnes.

3.   Mon oncle et ma tante (la planche à neige) _____ .

4.   Je (le soccer) _____ à l'école.

5.   Tous les jours, nous (le hockey) _____ après l'école.

6.   Au Canada, nous (le canotage) _____ dans les lacs.

7.   Tu (la plongée sous-marine) _____ .

8.   Toi et ta sœur, vous (le tennis) _____ le samedi.

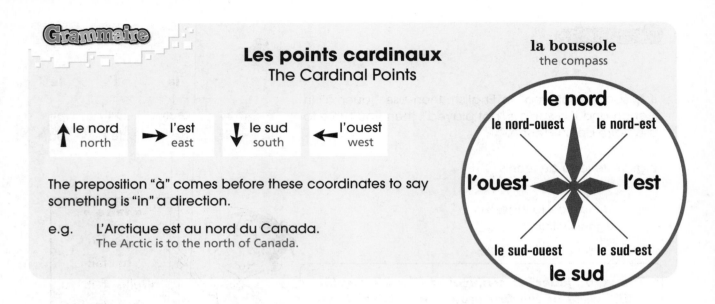

Grammaire

Les points cardinaux
The Cardinal Points

la boussole
the compass

↑ le nord north → l'est east ↓ le sud south ← l'ouest west

The preposition "à" comes before these coordinates to say something is "in" a direction.

e.g. L'Arctique est au nord du Canada.
The Arctic is to the north of Canada.

le nord
le nord-ouest   le nord-est
l'ouest   l'est
le sud-ouest   le sud-est
le sud

E. **Dessinez votre portrait dans le cercle. Ensuite répondez aux questions.**
Draw yourself in the circle. Then answer the questions.

1. Où est le parc?

Le parc est au _____-_____ de moi.

2. Où est l'hôpital?

_____

3. Où est l'aéroport?

_____

4. Où est le restaurant?

_____

5. Tu es au parc. Où sont les toilettes?

_____

6. Tu es à l'hôpital. Où est le parking?

_____

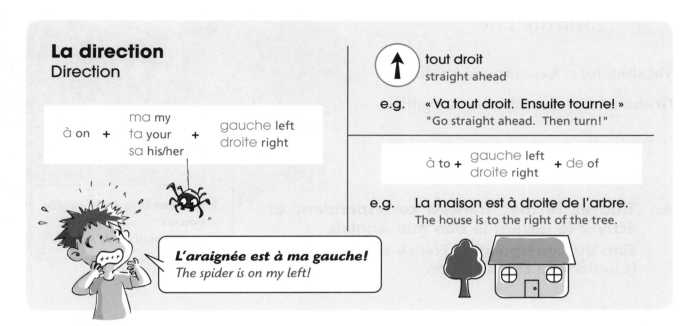

La direction
Direction

à on **+** ma my / ta your / sa his/her **+** gauche left / droite right

L'araignée est à ma gauche!
The spider is on my left!

↑ tout droit
straight ahead

e.g. « Va tout droit. Ensuite tourne! »
"Go straight ahead. Then turn!"

à to **+** gauche left / droite right **+** de of

e.g. La maison est à droite de l'arbre.
The house is to the right of the tree.

F. À l'aide de l'image, remplissez les tirets avec la bonne direction.
With the help of the picture, fill in the blanks with the correct directions.

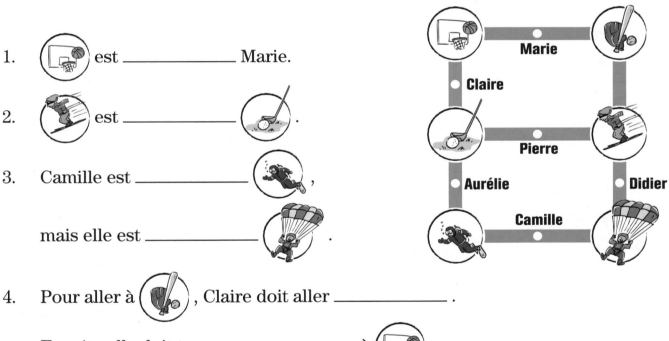

1. est _____ Marie.

2. est _____ .

3. Camille est _____ ,

   mais elle est _____ .

4. Pour aller à , Claire doit aller _____ .

   Ensuite elle doit tourner _____ à .

5. Marie veut aller à . Elle doit aller _____ .

   Ensuite elle doit tourner _____ à . Elle doit continuer

   _____ jusqu'à .

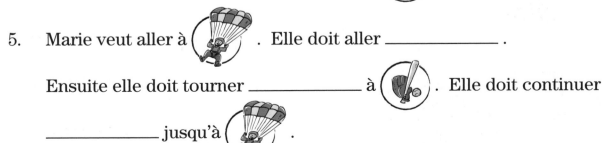

La vie marine

Marine Life

Vocabulaire : Les animaux marins

Grammaire : Les adjectifs irréguliers

Vous êtes une jolie petite méduse!
You are a pretty little jellyfish!

A. Trouvez le mot français correspondant et écrivez-le devant le bon mot anglais.

Find the corresponding French word and write it beside the English word.

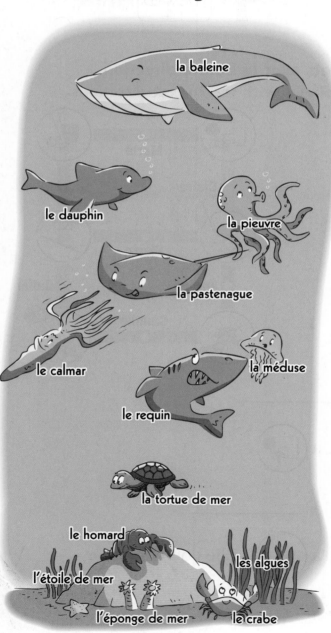

la baleine

le dauphin

la pieuvre

la pastenague

le calmar

la méduse

le requin

la tortue de mer

le homard

les algues

l'étoile de mer

l'éponge de mer   le crabe

1. __la calmar__ the squid
   luh kahl·mahr

2. __la pastenague__ the stingray
   lah pahs·tuh·nahg

3. __le crabe__ the crab
   luh krahb

4. __la baleine__ the whale
   lah bah·lehn

5. __l'etoile de mer__ the starfish
   leh·twahl duh mehr

6. __la dauphin__ the dolphin
   luh doh·fahn

7. __le requin__ the shark
   luh ruh·kahn

8. __le hormard__ the lobster
   luh oh·mahr

9. __la tortue de mer__ the sea turtle
   lah tohr·tew duh mehr

10. __réponge de mer__ the sea sponge
    leh·pohnj duh mehr

11. __les algues__ the seaweed
    leh zahlg

12. __la méduse__ the jellyfish
    lah meh·dewz

13. __la pieuvre__ the octopus
    lah pyuhvr

B. Mettez les animaux marins dans les bons groupes.
Put the sea animals into the correct groups.

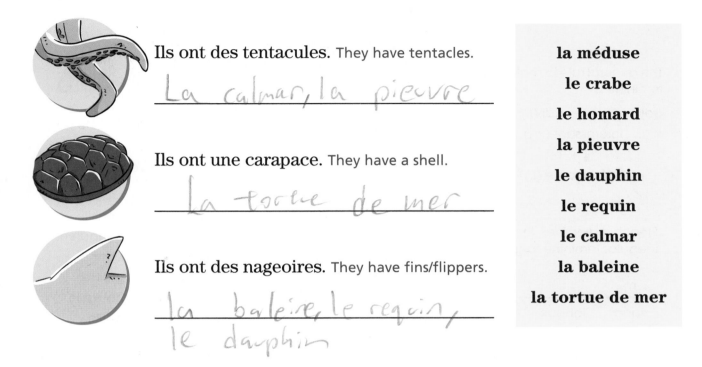

Ils ont des tentacules. They have tentacles.

La calmar, la pieuvre

Ils ont une carapace. They have a shell.

La tortue de mer

Ils ont des nageoires. They have fins/flippers.

la baleine, le requin, le dauphin

la méduse
le crabe
le homard
la pieuvre
le dauphin
le requin
le calmar
la baleine
la tortue de mer

C. Écrivez le nom de chaque organisme. Ensuite reliez-le au bon mot anglais.
Write the name of each life form. Then match it with the correct English word.

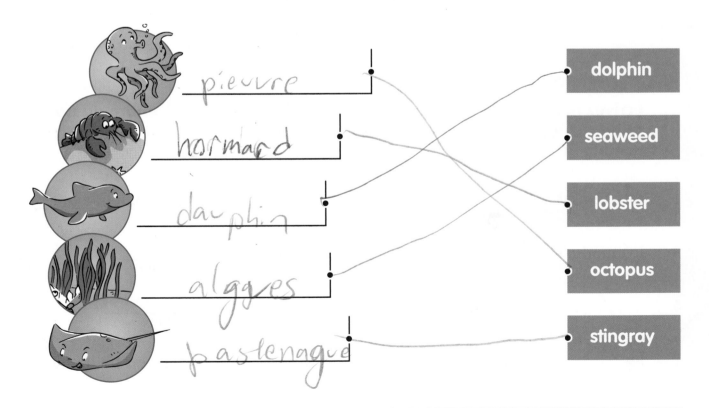

pieuvre

homard

dauphin

algues

pastenague

dolphin

seaweed

lobster

octopus

stingray

Les adjectifs irréguliers
Irregular Adjectives

> *French adjectives must agree in gender and number with the noun they describe.*

The general rule to make adjectives feminine is:

adj.(m.) + -e → adj.(f.)

e.g.   intéressant (m.)

↓ + -e

intéressant**e** (f.)

French adjectives that take an irregular feminine form are:

m.	f.	
long	longue	long
public	publique	public
doux	douce	soft
faux	fausse	false
favori	favorite	favourite
sec	sèche	dry
blanc	blanche	white

The following table shows the singular endings for masculine and feminine adjectives:

m.	f.	exemple	
-el	-elle	cruel	→ cruelle
-il	-ille	gentil	→ gentille
-en	-enne	canadien	→ canadienne
-on	-onne	bon	→ bonne
-os	-osse	gros	→ grosse
-eau	-elle	nouveau	→ nouvelle
-ou	-olle	mou	→ molle
-eur/eux	-euse	heureux	→ heureuse
-e	doesn't change	triste	→ triste

The general rule to make adjectives plural is:

adj.(sg.) + -s → adj.(pl.)

e.g. intéressante (f. sg.)

↓ + -s

intéressante**s** (f.pl.)

sg.	pl.
-eau	-eaux
-eu	-eux
-ou	-oux
-s/x	doesn't change

D.   Écrivez la bonne forme de l'adjectif selon le genre et le nombre du nom.
Write the correct form of the adjective depending on the gender and the number of the noun.

1.   une femme _____
         italien

2.   une _____ baleine
           beau

3.   les méduses _____
              mou

4.   les crabes _____
             frais

5.   un _____ requin
          gros

6.   une algue _____
             doux

7.   les _____ homards
          beau

8.   une _____ étoile de mer
            gentil

E. Écrivez la bonne forme de l'adjectif.
Write the correct form of the adjective.

Bonjour! Je m'appelle Samuel. J'habite au bord d'un

_____ (grand) océan _____ (ancien). Ma

mère m'apprend à faire de la plongée sous-marine. J'ai

une bouteille de plongée₁ _____ (blanc) et des palmes₂

_____ (gris). Le fond₃ de l'océan est très _____ (sombre₄) parce

qu'il est _____ (profond₅). J'aime regarder les pastenagues avec leurs

ventres (m.) _____ (blanc) et _____ (doux). Elles ne sont jamais

_____ (sec); au contraire, elles sont toujours _____ (mouillé₆)

parce qu'elles ne sortent jamais de l'eau. Ma mère, elle aime recueillir₇ de

_____ (gros) crustacés₈ comme des crabes et des crevettes. Parfois, nous

faisons de la pêche sous-marine ensemble. Les poissons que nous pêchons sont

très _____ (délicieux) et _____ (délicat). Quand nous rentrons

chez nous, nous faisons cuire₉ les poissons et les

crustacés _____ (frais).

Ma mère aime bien cette

partie₁₀ de la journée!

1. *une bouteille de plongée* : a scuba tank
2. *une palme* : a flipper
3. *le fond* : the bottom
4. *sombre* : dark
5. *profond* : deep
6. *mouillé* : wet
7. *recueillir* : to gather
8. *le crustacé* : shellfish
9. *faire cuire* : to cook
10. *une partie* : a part

La position des adjectifs
The Position of Adjectives

noun	adjective		adjective	noun

masculin	féminin	masculin	féminin
bas	basse	beau (bel+vowel)	belle
*blanc	blanche	bon	bonne
franc	franche	mauvais	mauvaise
frais	fraîche	joli	jolie
sec	sèche	gentil	gentille
roux	rousse	long	longue
faux	fausse	court	courte
public	publique	grand	grande
fou	folle	gros	grosse
mou	molle	petit	petite
cruel	cruelle	premier	première
drôle	drôle	dernier	dernière
		nouveau (nouvel+vowel)	nouvelle
		vieux (vieil+vowel)	vieille

* Most colour adjectives go after the noun.

In French, most adjectives (especially the longer ones) go after the noun!

e.g.
une fille fantastique
un journal hebdomadaire

However, in some cases (usually when the adjective has only one syllable), they are placed before the noun.

e.g.
une belle fille
un gros journal

F. **Ajoutez l'adjectif à la bonne place dans la phrase avec « ^ ».**
Add the given adjective in the correct place in the sentence with "^".

1. Je mange beaucoup de légumes. (frais)

2. Elle portent des jupes. (courtes)

3. Nous portons des chandails de hockey. (nouveaux)

4. Mon chien n'aime plus courir dans le parc. (vieux)

5. La robe est dans le magasin. (jolie ; petit)

6. Ils vont bâtir un hôtel à côté du pont. (nouvel ; petit)

G. Écrivez une phrase pour chaque image en utilisant les adjectifs contraires.
Write a sentence for each picture by using opposite adjectives.

grande

cruel

premier

longues

A La baleine est ___*grande*___ , elle n'est pas petite.

B _____

C _____

D _____

H. Remplissez les tirets avec le bon adjectif comparatif.
Fill in the blanks with the correct comparative adjectives.

1. La baleine est __*plus*__ gentille __*que*__ le requin.
    <small>nicer than</small>

2. La pastenague est __*moins amusent*__ __*que*__ le dauphin.
    <small>less funny than</small>

3. La pieuvre est __*plus grande*__ __*que*__ le calmar.
    <small>larger than</small>

4. Le homard est __*moins beau que*__ l'étoile de mer.
    <small>less pretty than</small>

5. La tortue est _____ la crevette.
    <small>older than</small>

plus + adj. + que
↳ *more...than*

moins + adj. + que
↳ *less...than*

L'impératif

The Imperative

Révision :   Les verbes réguliers en « -ER »,
« -IR » et « -RE »

L'impératif

Expressions :   « Arrête de... »

Arrête de me regarder! Mange!
Stop looking at me! Eat!

A.   Copiez les mots.
Copy the words.

Les verbes du...

1ᵉʳ groupe « **-ER** »	2ᵉ groupe « **-IR** »	3ᵉ groupe « **-RE** »
parler to talk	**choisir** to choose	**répondre** to answer
pahr·leh	*shwah·zeer*	*reh·pohndr*
sauter to jump	**finir** to finish	**attendre** to wait
soh·teh	*fee·neer*	*ah·taandr*
manger to eat	**remplir** to fill	**rendre** to return
maan·jeh	*raam·pleer*	*raandr*
nager to swim	**obéir** to obey	**entendre** to hear
nah·jeh	*oh·beh·yeer*	*aan·taandr*
marcher to walk	**réussir** to succeed	**défendre** to defend
mahr·sheh	*reh·ew·seer*	*deh·faandr*
chanter to sing	**nourrir** to feed	**vendre** to sell
shaan·teh	*noo·reer*	*vaandr*

Les terminaisons
Verb Endings

	« -ER »	« -IR »	« -RE »
je	-e	-is	-s
tu	-es	-is	-s
il/elle	-e	-it	—
nous	-*(e)ons	-issons	-ons
vous	-ez	-issez	-ez
ils/elles	-ent	-issent	-ent

* *"-eons" is only used in the first person plural of verbs ending with "-GER".*

Je vends des œufs.
I sell eggs.

Je mange des œufs.
I eat eggs.

B. Remplissez les tirets avec la bonne forme du verbe donné.
Fill in the blanks with the correct form of the given verbs.

1. Je _finis_ (finir) toujours mes devoirs.

2. Nous _mangeons_ (manger) beaucoup de légumes.

3. Est-ce que tu _rends_ (rendre) les livres à la bibliothèque?

4. Vous _réussissez_ (réussir) dans la vie.

5. Les lapins _sautent_ (sauter) très haut.

6. Ils _obéissent_ (obéir) à leurs parents.

7. Tu _réponds_ (répondre) aux questions.

8. Tu _remplis_ (remplir) le verre avec du jus.

9. Je _parle_ (parler) à mes amis.

10. Il _défend_ (défendre) sa sœur.

L'impératif
The Imperative

The imperative expresses a command or a request. The imperative is used only in the 2nd person singular (tu), 1st person plural (nous), and 2nd person plural (vous). In the imperative, the subject pronouns are not expressed.

	1er groupe « -ER »	2e groupe « -IR »	3e groupe « -RE »
tu you (sg.)	Mange ✗!* Eat!	Finis! Finish!	Réponds! Answer!
nous we (pl.)	Mangeons! Let's eat!	Finissons! Let's finish!	Répondons! Let's answer!
vous you (pl./polite "tu")	Mangez! Eat!	Finissez! Finish!	Répondez! Answer!

* In the imperative, "-ER" verbs do not take the usual "-s" ending in the 2nd person singular.

Mangeons!

C. **Identifiez la personne qui reçoit la commande. Écrivez la bonne lettre dans la case.**

Identify to whom the command is addressed. Write the correct letter in the box.

A — tu
nous — B
C — vous

C	Répondez à la question!
A	Lave-toi!
A	Choisis un livre!
B	Finissons le cours!
B	Écoutons les annonces!

D. Remplissez les tirets avec la bonne forme du verbe.
Fill in the blanks with the correct form of the verbs.

Martin,

1. ___*Finis*___ tes devoirs!
   finish

2. _____ tes vêtements!
   wash

3. ___*Nourris*___ le chien!
   feed

4. ___*Rends*___ les livres à la
   return

   bibliothèque!

5. ___*Mange*___ le gâteau!
   eat

6. ___*Chansez*___ la chanson!
   sing (vous)

7. _____ aux questions!
   answer (vous)

8. ___*Choisissez*___ la bonne réponse!
   choose (vous)

9. _____ de la limonade cet été!
   let's sell

10. ___*Finissons*___ le lait au chocolat!
    let's finish

11. ___*Remplissez*___ les tirets avec la bonne forme.
    fill in (vous)   the blanks with the correct form.

L'impératif et la négation
The Imperative and the Negative

Use negative adverbs (ne...pas/jamais, etc.) with the imperative to command or tell someone not to do something.

Negative Adverbs:

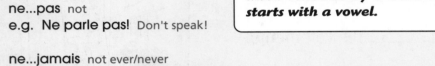

- **ne...pas** not
  e.g. **Ne parle pas!** Don't speak!

  > **Remember! "Ne" becomes "n'" when followed by a word that starts with a vowel.**

- **ne...jamais** not ever/never
  e.g. **Ne nagez jamais dans le lac!** Don't ever/Never swim in the lake!

- **ne...plus** not anymore/no more
  e.g. **Ne regardons plus la télévision!** Let's not watch TV anymore!

E. **Écrivez les phrases impératives au négatif.**
Write the imperative sentences in the negative.

1. Lave mon chandail à la machine! (ne...pas)

   Ne lave pas mon chandail à la machine!

2. Nageons dans le lac! (ne...jamais)

   Ne nageons jamais dans le lac!

3. Jouez au football américain sans casques! (ne...jamais)

   Ne jouez jamais au football américain sans casques!

4. Mange des bonbons! (ne...plus)

Expressions

En anglais : In English	En français : In French
"Stop (verb) + '-ing'." "Let's stop (verb) + '-ing'."	« Arrête/Arrêtez de + infinitif » « Arrêtons de + infinitif »

Arrêtez de rire!
Stop laughing!

F. Commandez aux gens de s'arrêter.
Command the person to stop what they are doing.

1. Jacqueline parle. (tu)

    Ne parles pas

2. Nous étudions. (nous)

    Ne étudions pas

3. Manon saute sur son lit. (tu)

    Ne sautes pas sur son lit

4. Marc et Julie nagent dans la piscine. (vous)

    Ne nagez pas dans la piscine

5. Elles salissent leurs robes. (vous)

    Ne salissez pas leurs robes

6. Le chat marche sur le canapé. (tu)

    Ne marche pas sur le canapé

7. Samuel et Joseph écoutent aux portes. (vous)

    Ne écoutez pas aux portes

La technologie et l'Internet

Technology and the Internet

Vocabulaire : Le jargon informatique

Grammaire : L'interrogatif et l'inversion

A. Copiez les mots. ~~NO~~
Copy the words.

Je peux voir ma famille sur l'écran!
I can see my family on the screen!

l'ordinateur (m.) the computer

l'ordinateur
lohr·dee·nah·tuhr

A l'imprimante (f.)
the printer

l'imprimante
lahm·pree·maant

B l'écran (m.)
the screen

l'écran
leh·kraan

C le clavier
the keyboard

le clavier
luh klah·vyeh

D la souris
the mouse

la souris
lah soo·ree

l'icône (f.)
the icon

l'icône
lee·kohn

l'Internet (m.)
the Internet

l'internet
lahn·tehr·neht

la page d'accueil
the home page

la page d'accueil
lah pahj dah·kuhy

l'aide (f.)
help

l'aide
lehd

le site Web
the website

le site Web
luh seet wehb

le curseur
the cursor

le curseur
luh kuhr·suhr

le message
the message

le message
luh meh·sahj

le courriel
the e-mail

le courriel
luh koo·ryehl

le blogue
the blog

le blogue
luh blohg

Tuesday

Les verbes

> *"Télécharger" is conjugated like "manger/nager".*
> *1ʳᵉ personne plurielle → téléchargeons*

« envoyer »

j'envoie

tu envoies

il/elle envoie

nous envoyons

vous envoyez

ils/elles envoient

envoyer
to send

envoyer

aan·vwah·yeh

rechercher
to search

rechercher

ruh·shehr·sheh

télécharger
to download

télécharger

teh·leh·shahr·jeh

taper
to type

taper

tah·peh

surfer
to surf

surfer

suhr·feh

bloguer
to blog

bloguer

bloh·geh

cliquer
to click

cliquer

klee·keh

annuler
to cancel

annuler

ah·new·leh

imprimer
to print

imprimer

ahm·pree·meh

B. Complétez les phrases avec les bons mots.
Complete the sentences with the correct words.

1. Béatrice _____tape_____ (types) sur ____le clavier____ (keyboard).

2. Marie _____surfe_____ (surfs) sur ____l'internet____ (the Internet).

3. Stéphane _____clique_____ (clicks) sur ____l'icône____ (the icon).

4. Vous _____tapez_____ (type) votre mot de passe.
    moh duh pahs
    password

5.
    > J' ____envoye____ (send)
    >
    > ____le courriel____ (an e-mail) à mon ami.

Poser une question avec l'inversion
Asking a Question with Inversion

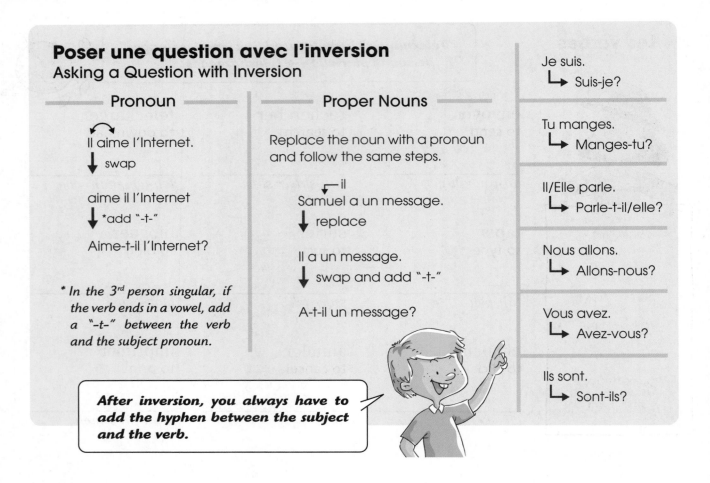

Pronoun

Il aime l'Internet.
↓ swap

aime il l'Internet
↓ *add "-t-"

Aime-t-il l'Internet?

* In the 3rd person singular, if the verb ends in a vowel, add a "-t-" between the verb and the subject pronoun.

After inversion, you always have to add the hyphen between the subject and the verb.

Proper Nouns

Replace the noun with a pronoun and follow the same steps.

┌─ il
Samuel a un message.
↓ replace

Il a un message.
↓ swap and add "-t-"

A-t-il un message?

Je suis.
↳ Suis-je?

Tu manges.
↳ Manges-tu?

Il/Elle parle.
↳ Parle-t-il/elle?

Nous allons.
↳ Allons-nous?

Vous avez.
↳ Avez-vous?

Ils sont.
↳ Sont-ils?

C. **Changez les phrases en questions avec l'inversion.**
Change the sentences into questions using inversion.

1. L'étudiant a besoin d'aide.

   A-t-il besoin d'aide

2. Moi et Luc cherchons le mot clé sur le site Web.

   Cherchons ils le mot clé sur le site web

3. Son adresse électronique est vjoor245@popular.com.

   Adresse-son électronique est _____

4. Zoé télécharge ses devoirs du site Web.

   Télécharge A-t-il ses devoirs du site web

L'adjectif interrogatif « quel »
The Interrogative Adjective "Quel"

« **Quel** » what/which

- can be followed by a noun
  e.g. Quelle saison préfères-tu? Which season do you prefer?

- can be followed by "être + noun"
  e.g. Quelle est ta saison préférée? What is your favourite season?

- must always agree in gender and number with the noun that follows

Les différentes formes de « quel »

quel (m.sg.)

quelle (f.sg.)

quels (m.pl.)

quelles (f.pl.)

> **Quel moule préfères-tu?**
> *Which mould do you prefer?*

> **Je préfère l'étoile. Quel est ton moule préféré?**
> *I prefer the star. Which mould do you prefer?*

D. **Remplissez les tirets avec la bonne forme de « quel ».**
Fill in the blanks with the correct form of "quel".

1. _____quel_____ mot de passe (m.) choisis-tu?

2. _____quels_____ est ton courriel?

3. _____quels_____ imprimantes avez-vous à la maison?

4. _____quel_____ site Web visites-tu régulièrement?

5. _____quelle_____ souris utilise-t-elle?

6. _____quelles_____ blogues aiment-ils les plus?

7. _____quels_____ message envoyons-nous?

8. _____quelles_____ sont les adresses (f.pl.) les plus importantes?

E. **Complétez les phrases. Ensuite répondez aux questions.**
Complete the sentences. Then answer the questions.

1. ___Quel___ est le courriel de Jérôme?

Le courriel de Jérôme est ___jêôhe gmail.com___.

2. ___Quel___ est l'adresse de la page d'accueil?
___l'adresse de la page d'accueil est___ —

3. ___Quelle___ est la couleur principale de la page?
___Le coleur principle est rouge.___

4. Sur ___quelle___ image (f.) le curseur se trouve-t-il?
___Le image se trouve-t-il___

5. ___Quel___ est le mot de passe de Jérôme?
___Le mot de passe est v3p___

6. Jérôme envoie le courriel à ___quelle___ adresse (f.)?
___Jérôme envoie le courriel à 0234 street___

F. Répondez aux questions avec « oui/non » à l'aide de l'image en question E.

Answer the questions with "Oui/Non" with the help of the picture in question E.

1. Le garçon crie-t-il « Envoyez! »?

   Oui , le garçon crie « Envoyez! ».

2. Jérôme, est-il sur la page d'accueil?

   Non, Jérôme ne sur pas la page d'accueil

3. Jérôme, clique-t-il sur l'icône de l'imprimante?

   Non, il ne clique pas sur l'icône de l'imprimante

4. Jérôme, envoie-t-il le message?

   Oui, il envoie le message

5. Le garçon, est-il à gauche du message?

   Oui, il est à je gauche du message

6. Le mot de passe, est-il « mélodie333 »?

   Non, le mot de passe ne pas «mélodie333»

7. Le message, a-t-il un sujet?

   Oui, le message a un sujet

8. Jérôme, annule-t-il le message?

   Non, il ne annule pas le message

Le monde

The World

Vocabulaire : Les pays du monde

Grammaire : Les prépositions « à » et « en » avec les pays

Compréhension : Les Canadiens célèbres

> *Je vais aller partout dans le monde!*
> *I'm going to go all around the world.*

A. Copiez les noms des pays.
Copy the names of the countries.

la carte du monde the world map

_____

lah kahrt dew mohnd

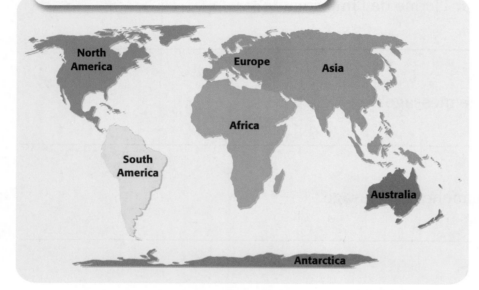

North America

Europe

Asia

Africa

South America

Australia

Antarctica

un pays
a country

_____

euhn peh·yee

la nationalité
nationality

_____

lah nah·syoh·nah·lee·teh

l'Amérique du Nord
North America

le Canada
Canada

_____

luh kah·nah·dah

le Mexique
Mexico

_____

luh mehk·seek

les États-Unis
the United States

_____

leh zeh·tah·zew·nee

la Jamaïque
Jamaica

_____

lah jah·mah·eek

l'Australie
Australia

_____

lohs·trah·lee

l'Antarctique
Antarctica

_____

laan·tahrk·teek

l'Asie Asia

le Japon	l'Inde	la Chine
Japan	India	China
luh jah·pohn	*lahnd*	*lah sheen*
la Russie	Israël	la Corée du Sud
Russia	Israel	South Korea
lah rew·see	*eez·rah·ehl*	*lah koh·reh dew sewd*

l'Amérique du Sud South America

le Brésil	l'Argentine
Brazil	Argentina
luh breh·zeel	*lahr·jaan·teen*
la Colombie	le Pérou
Colombia	Peru
lah koh·lohm·bee	*luh peh·roo*
l'Équateur	le Venezuela
Ecuador	Venezuela
leh·kwah·tuhr	*luh veh·neh·zweh·lah*

l'Europe Europe

l'Angleterre	la France
England	France
laan·gluh·tehr	*lah fraans*
l'Allemagne	l'Italie
Germany	Italy
lahl·mahny	*lee·tah·lee*
l'Irlande	l'Espagne
Ireland	Spain
leer·laand	*lehs·pahny*

l'Afrique Africa

le Maroc	le Kenya	le Zimbabwe
Morocco	Kenya	Zimbabwe
luh mah·rohk	*luh keh·nyah*	*luh zeem·bahb·weh*
l'Afrique du Sud	l'Algérie	l'Égypte
South Africa	Algeria	Egypt
lah·freek dew sewd	*lahl·jeh·ree*	*leh·jeept*

In French, the names of countries begin with a capital letter. However, nationality adjectives begin with a lower case letter.

Nationality adjectives, like descriptive adjectives, have both a masculine and a feminine form. They always agree in number and gender with the noun they describe.

un citoyen **canadien**
a Canadian citizen

B. **Complétez la grille des adjectifs. Ensuite reliez chaque paire d'adjectifs au bon pays.**
Complete the nationality adjective table. Then match each pair of adjectives with the correct country.

Les adjectifs de nationalité

	m.	f.
-ien → -ienne	canadien	canadienne
	australien	
		brésilienne
+e	mexicain	mexicaine
	chinois	
	kényan	
		japonaise
		allemande
	anglais	
		espagnole
no change	russe	
		suisse
	belge	

Les pays

- l'Allemagne
- le Japon
- la Russie
- la Belgique
- la Chine
- l'Espagne
- l'Australie
- le Canada
- le Brésil
- le Kenya
- l'Angleterre
- la Suisse
- le Mexique

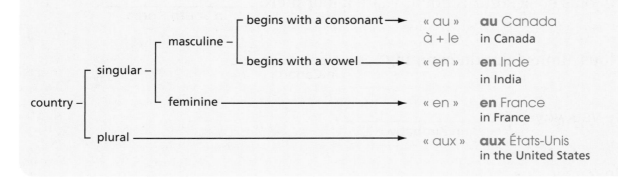

Les prépositions « à » et « en »
The Prepositions "à" and "en"

The prepositions "à" and "en" are put before the names of countries to express location "in" that country.

à/en ➕ a country

country —
- singular —
  - masculine —
    - begins with a consonant ⟶ « au » **au** Canada
      - à + le — in Canada
    - begins with a vowel ⟶ « en » **en** Inde
      - in India
  - feminine ⟶ « en » **en** France
    - in France
- plural ⟶ « aux » **aux** États-Unis
  - in the United States

C. **Remplissez les tirets avec la bonne préposition.**
Fill in the blanks with the correct prepositions.

1. Sophie habite _____ Canada avec ses parents.

2. Nous allons faire de la natation dans la mer du Nord, _____ Belgique.

3. J'aime bien faire du surf _____ Australie.

4. Cet été, je vais aller au camp de foot _____ Brésil.

5. La reine habite _____ Angleterre.

6. La ville de New York est _____ États-Unis.

7. Moi et ma famille, nous allons _____ France.

8. Pour mes vacances, je préfère aller _____ Italie.

9. _____ Antarctique, il y a des baleines bleues.

D. **Remplissez les tirets avec la bonne préposition et le bon nom du pays.**
Fill in the blanks with the correct prepositions and country names.

1. Mon père et moi, nous habitons _____ .
   in Switzerland

2. Nicolas et sa sœur rendent visite à leur mère _____ .
   in South Korea

3. Nous allons faire du camping _____ .
   in Canada

4. Je vais voyager _____ .
   in Zimbabwe

5. Je mange des tapas _____ .
   in Spain

6. Ils regardent les peintures au musée du Louvre, _____ .
   in France

7. Nous jouons de la flûte de Pan _____ .
   in Peru

8. Je bois du café _____ .
   in Colombia

9. Elles jouent au cricket _____ .
   in England

10.
   Vous allez visiter les pyramides

   _____ .
   in Egypt

E. **Remplissez les tirets avec le bon pronom. Ensuite répondez aux questions.**
Fill in the blanks with the correct pronouns. Then answer the questions.

————— **Joseph-Armand Bombardier** —————
« 16 avril 1907 – 18 février 1964 »

La marque Bombardier est connue à travers₁ le monde.

C'est le canadien Joseph-Armand Bombardier, né ——————

Québec (m.), qui a fondé₂ la compagnie Bombardier. Il était₃

aussi l'inventeur₄ de la motoneige₅. Aujourd'hui, Bombardier

fabrique plus que des motoneiges! Les services de transport

qui portent la marque Bombardier se trouvent —————— France, —————— Mexique,

—————— Inde, —————— Japon, —————— Corée du Sud et même —————— Canada!

N'êtes-vous pas fiers₆ d'être canadien comme cette compagnie prospère?

1. Où est-ce que Joseph-Armand Bombardier est né?

   _____

2. Quelle est sa nationalité?

   _____

3. Où trouve-t-on les services de transport qui portent la marque Bombardier?

_____

1. à travers : across	*2. fonder : to found/establish*	*3. était : was*
4. l'inventeur : the inventor	*5. la motoneige : the snowmobile*	*6. fier, fière : proud*

Au jardin

In the Garden

Vocabulaire : Mots pour faire du jardinage

Révision : « Est-ce que... »

Grammaire : Les pronoms et les adverbes interrogatifs

A. Copiez les mots.
Copy the words.

> **Qu'est-ce que vous aimez faire dans votre jardin?**
> *What do you like to do in your garden?*

Dans mon jardin il y a...

l'herbe (f.) the grass	**les fleurs** the flowers	**le ver** the worm	**la brouette** the wheelbarrow
lehrb	*leh fluhr*	*luh vehr*	*lah broo·eht*
la terre the earth	**la pelle** the shovel	**le gazon** the lawn	**l'arrosoir (m.)** the watering can
lah tehr	*lah pehl*	*luh gah·zohn*	*lah·roh·zwahr*

Dans mon jardin j'aime...

tondre to mow

tohndr

arroser to water

ah·roh·zeh

pousser to grow

poo·seh

cueillir* to gather

kuh·yeer

> **"Cueillir" is conjugated like an "-ER" verb.*

arracher to rip out

ah·rah·sheh

remplir to fill

raam·pleer

planter to plant

plaan·teh

B. **Remplissez les tirets pour compléter les paroles des personnages.**
Fill in the blanks to complete what the people are saying.

Aujourd'hui, je 1._____ dans mon
to go down (au présent)

2._____ pour 3._____
garden   to mow

4._____ . Je 5._____
the grass   to do (au présent)

attention à ne pas 6._____
to rip out

7._____ . J'aime bien
the flowers

8._____
to work

au jardin.

Nous aimons 9._____
to plant

les fleurs. Nous aimons aussi

10._____ les fleurs. Mais
to look

Sarah, elle aime 11._____
to gather

les fleurs le plus.

Demain, je vais descendre dans le jardin

pour 12._____ les fleurs. Je vais
to water

13._____ mon gros 14._____
to fill   watering can

gris avec de l'eau. J'aime 15._____ 16._____ sur 17._____ .
to watch   the worms   the earth

Les vers de terre aident les fleurs et 18._____ à 19._____ .
the grass   to grow

Poser une question avec « est-ce que »
Asking a Question with "est-ce que"

> In French, you can turn any sentence into a question by putting "est-ce que" at the beginning.

e.g.   Le chat est noir et blanc. ◄── sentence

Est-ce que le chat est noir et blanc? ◄── question
Is the cat black and white?

C.   Transformez les questions suivantes en questions avec « est-ce que ».
Change the following into questions with "est-ce que".

1.   La fleur pousse-t-elle dans le jardin?

_____ la fleur pousse dans le jardin?

2.   Manon pousse-t-elle la brouette?

_____

3.   Arrosons-nous le jardin?

_____

4.   Remplis-tu l'arrosoir?

_____

5.   Portes-tu des gants de jardinage?

_____

6.   As-tu faim Minou?

_____

Les adverbes interrogatifs
Interrogative Adverbs

Quand est-ce que nous allons planter les graines?
When

Comment est-ce que tu tonds le gazon?
How

Combien de vers est-ce que tu as?
How many

Où est-ce qu'il va planter les tomates?
Where

Pourquoi est-ce qu'elle pousse la brouette?
Why

**Quand · Comment
Combien de · Où · Pourquoi**

These interrogative adverbs can also be placed before questions formed with inversion.

D. **Encerclez l'adverbe interrogatif correspondant aux mots soulignés.**
Circle the interrogative adverb that corresponds to the underlined word.

1. Marie plante des légumes <u>dans le jardin</u>.　　Où / Qui / Comment

2. Je plante <u>trois fleurs</u>.　　Qui / Où / Combien de

3. Le radis pousse <u>sous la terre</u>.　　Quand / Comment / Où

4. Il tond le gazon <u>chaque semaine</u>.　　Quand / Où / Pourquoi

5. J'aime arracher les carottes <u>avec mes mains</u>.　　Combien de / Où / Comment

6. <u>Les garçons</u> arrosent les plantes.　　Quand / Qui / Comment

7. Il n'aime pas la pomme <u>parce qu'elle n'est pas mûre</u>.　　Quand / Où / Pourquoi

Les pronoms interrogatifs
Interrogative Pronouns

« Qui » who/whom (person) ────────

Subject (who) Qui? Qui est-ce qui?

> <u>Marie</u> regarde Paul.
> subject (person)

- **Qui** regarde Paul?

- **Qui est-ce qui** regarde Paul?

Object (whom) ────────

Qui + Inversion   Qui est-ce que?

> Marie regarde **<u>Paul</u>**.
> object (person)

- **Qui** regarde-t-elle?

- **Qui est-ce qu'**elle regarde?

« Que » what (thing) ────────

Subject (what) Qu'est-ce qui?

> <u>Le chat</u> danse.
> subject (thing)

- **Qu'est-ce qui** danse?

Object (what) ────────

Que + Inversion

Qu'est-ce que?

> Marie regarde **<u>la télévision</u>**.
> object (thing)

- **Que** regarde-t-elle?

- **Qu'est-ce qu'**elle regarde?

E. **Encerclez le rôle grammatical du mot souligné. Ensuite posez une question dont le mot souligné est la réponse.**

Circle the grammatical role of the underlined word. Then ask a question about the underlined word.

1. Marie mange <u>son repas</u>.   sujet/objet

   Question : _____

2. <u>Marie</u> embrasse son chat.   sujet/objet

   Question : _____

3. Paul aime <u>sa mère</u>.   sujet/objet

   Question : _____

F. **Écrivez les questions du journaliste selon les réponses de Murielle.**
Write the journalist's questions based on Murielle's answers.

1. **J** : _____ couleurs différentes est-ce que vous avez dans votre jardin?

   Le jardin de Murielle gagne le premier prix!

   M : J'ai trois couleurs différentes dans mon jardin : le jaune, le rouge et le violet.

2. **J** : _____

   _____

   M : Je plante mes graines en avril.

3. **J** : _____

   M : Mon jardin est derrière ma maison.

4. **J** : _____

   M : Je plante toujours des roses parce que j'aime la couleur rouge.

5. **J** : _____

   M : J'arrose mes plantes avec un gros arrosoir.

6. **J** : _____

   M : Je cueille mes fleurs avec mes mains.

Unité 7 — La fête

The Party

Vocabulaire : Les articles de fête

Grammaire : Les adjectifs démonstratifs

> **Cette fête est géniale!**
> *This party is great!*

A. Copiez les mots.
Copy the words.

La nourriture Food

_____
lah noo·ree·tewr

A une boisson gazeuse

_____
ewn bwah·sohn gah·zuhz

B une pizza

_____
ewn peed·zah

C un hamburger

_____
euhn ahm·buhr·gehr

D des croustilles (f.)

_____
deh kroos·teey

E la crème glacée

_____
lah krehm glah·seh

F un gâteau

_____
euhn gah·toh

Pour s'amuser For Fun

_____
poor sah·mew·zeh

G un jeu vidéo

_____
euhn juh vee·deh·oh

H des ballons (m.)

_____
deh bah·lohn

I la musique

_____
lah mew·zeek

J un chapeau de fête

_____
euhn shah·poh duh feht

K un cadeau

_____
euhn kah·doh

L un film

_____
euhn feelm

Les articles de fête Party Supplies

leh zahr·teekl duh feht

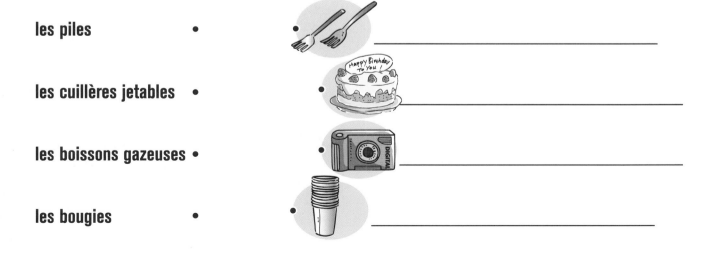

A des bougies (f.)

deh boo·jee

C des couteaux jetables

deh koo·toh juh·tahbl

E des assiettes jetables

deh zah·syeht juh·tahbl

G des serviettes (f.)

deh sehr·vyeht

B des fourchettes jetables

deh foor·shet juh·tahbl

D des cuillères jetables

deh kwee·yehr juh·tahbl

F des gobelets jetables

deh goh·bleh juh·tahbl

H un appareil photo

euhn ah·pah·rehy foh·toh

I des piles

deh peel

B. **Écrivez le nom des objets à droite. Ensuite reliez-les aux objets correspondants à gauche.**

Name the objects on the right. Then match them with the corresponding objects on the left.

les piles •

les cuillères jetables •

les boissons gazeuses •

les bougies •

Les adjectifs démonstratifs
Demonstrative Adjectives

singulier		pluriel
ce + nom (m.) e.g. **Ce** film est long. **cet** + nom (m. beginning with a vowel) e.g. **Cet** oiseau est beau.	**cette** + nom (f.) e.g. **Cette** musique est bonne.	**ces** + nom (pl.) e.g. **ces** films (m.pl.) **ces** oiseaux (m.pl.) **ces** musiques (f.pl.)

C. **Remplacez l'article souligné par le bon adjectif démonstratif.**
Replace the underlined article with the correct demonstrative adjective.

1. Nous allons à <u>la</u> fête. _____

2. L'étudiant aime <u>le</u> livre. _____

3. <u>Les</u> hamburgers sont fantastiques. _____

D. **Reformulez la phrase.**
Rephrase the sentence.

1. C'est un long film.

   _____ film est long.

2. C'est une belle photo.

   _____

3. C'est un grand cadeau.

   _____

4. Ce sont des longues bougies.

   _____

5. Ce sont des jeux amusants.

   _____

6. C'est une assiette jetable.

   _____

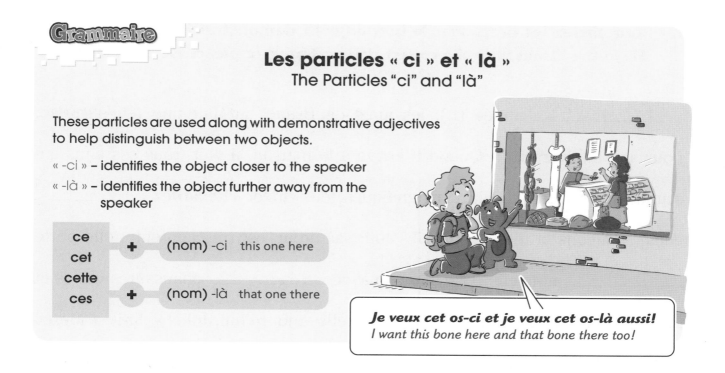

Grammaire

Les particles « ci » et « là »
The Particles "ci" and "là"

These particles are used along with demonstrative adjectives to help distinguish between two objects.

« -ci » – identifies the object closer to the speaker

« -là » – identifies the object further away from the speaker

ce		
cet	**+**	(nom) -ci this one here
cette		
ces	**+**	(nom) -là that one there

Je veux cet os-ci et je veux cet os-là aussi!
I want this bone here and that bone there too!

E.   Remplissez les tirets pour compléter les phrases.
Fill in the blanks to complete the sentences.

1.   Ces cadeaux-_____ sont à moi; _____ cadeaux-là sont à toi.

2.   _____ robe-_____ est jaune; _____ robe-là est rose.

3.   Ils jouent _____ jeux-ci; ils ne jouent jamais _____ jeux-_____ .

4.   _____ photos-là sont jolies; _____ photos-_____ sont mauvaises.

5.   Jacques peut manger _____ hamburger-là; il ne veut pas manger ce hamburger-_____ .

6.   _____ fourchettes-ci sont jetables mais _____ fourchettes-_____ ne sont pas jetables.

7.   Moi, j'ai fait _____ pizza-ci et mon frère a fait _____ pizza-_____ .

F. Remplissez les tirets avec le bon adjectif demonstratif ou possessif.
Fill in the blanks with the correct demonstrative or possessive adjectives.

_____ année (f.), les amis de Bruno ont fait une fête-surprise[1]

pour son anniversaire. Quand il arrive à la maison, il voit[2] tous ses amis qui

s'amusent avec _____ magnifiques[3] jeux vidéo. « Regardez _____

gens[4]! Faisons la fête! » crie-t-il. Julie, sa sœur, est très contente; elle porte

_____ nouvelle robe blanche avec _____ chaussures vertes et

_____ collier vert. « Tu est très belle aujourd'hui, Julie! » dit-il. « Merci,

Bruno! _____ fête est magnifique. J'adore _____ musique,

_____ gâteau et _____ bonbons! Je suis très contente que tu sois

né[5]! » _____ conversation (f.) avec sa sœur rend[6] Bruno très content. Tout

d'un coup[7], son cousin prend son bras et lui dit : « Ouvre _____ cadeau-là

il est de ma part! » « Wow! Regarde tous _____ cadeaux! _____

anniversaire (m.) est le meilleur! » dit Bruno. « _____ magicien, est-il pour

mon anniversaire aussi? » se demande-t-il. « _____ fête ne finit jamais! »

1. *faire une fête : to throw a party*
2. *voir : to see*
3. *magnifique : great*
4. *les gens : people*
5. *sois né : were born*
6. *rendre : to make*
7. *tout d'un coup : all of a sudden*

G. **Traduisez les phrases en anglais.**
Translate the sentences into English.

1. Cet animal-ci est très beau.

   _____

2. Ces lunettes de soleil sont rouges.

   _____

3. Ses films sont plus longs que ces films-ci.

   _____

4. Ce cadeau-là est à toi. Joyeux anniversaire!

   _____

> **Attention!**
>
> ces → *these*
> *seh*
> **e.g.** ces enfants *these kids*
>
> ses → *his/her*
> *seh*
> **e.g.** ses enfants *his/her kids*

H. **Traduisez les phrases en français.**
Translate the sentences into French.

1. This slice of pizza is mine; that one there is yours.

   _____

2. Ben wants this gift here; Paul wants that gift there.

   _____

3. We can play this music here but not that music there.

   _____

4. I don't like those balloons there; I like these balloons here.

   _____

5. These candies here are mine; those candies there are yours.

   _____

Quand? Où? Comment?

When? Where? How?

Où es-tu Charlie?
Where are you, Charlie?

Vocabulaire : Les adverbes de temps, lieu et manière

Grammaire : L'accord du temps verbal avec l'adverbe

Expressions : « Dans (<u>durée de temps</u>) »

A. Copiez les mots.
Copy the words.

Quand? When?

kaan

Les adverbes de temps

hier yesterday

ee·yehr

toujours always/still

too·joor

parfois sometimes

pahr·fwah

aujourd'hui today

oh·joor·dwee

maintenant now

mah·tuh·naan

souvent often

soo·vaan

demain tomorrow

duh·mahn

jamais never

jah·meh

rarement rarely

rahr·maan

Les adjectifs

dernier (m.) last

dehr·nyeh

dernière (f.)

dehr·nyehr

prochain (m.) next

proh·shahn

prochaine (f.)

proh·shehn

À la prochaine, grand-mère!
Gros bisous, Minou.
Until next time, Grandma!
Lots of love, Minou.

Les adverbes de lieu

Ici! Here!

_____
ee·see

Où? Where?

_____
oo

là there

_____
lah

loin (de) far (from)

_____
lwahn

partout everywhere

_____
pahr·too

près (de) close (to)

_____
preh

Les adverbes de manière

Comment? How?

_____
koh·maan

bien well

_____
byahn

mal badly

_____
mahl

vite fast/quickly

_____
veet

lentement slowly

_____
laant·maan

ensemble together

_____
aan·saambl

seul alone/by oneself

_____
suhl

B. Encerclez le bon adverbe de temps qui correspond à la phrase.
Circle the correct adverb of time that matches the sentence.

1. Je brosse mes dents...
    rarement / souvent

2. J'étudie le français...
    maintenant / prochain

3. Je vais aller au cinéma...
    demain / hier

4. Je rends visite à ma grand-mère...
    dernier / aujourd'hui

C. **Remplissez les tirets avec le bon adverbe de lieu.**
Fill in the blanks with the correct locative adverbs.

1.

_____ sont les bulles?

Elles sont _____ !

2.

_____ est ton vélo?

Il n'est pas _____ ,

il est _____ .

3.

_____ est le parc?

Il n'est pas loin d'ici.
Regarde!
Il est très _____ !

4.

_____ est Manon?

Elle est _____ !

Je suis _____ .

D. Répondez aux questions par des phrases complètes en utilisant les adverbes donnés.

Answer the questions in complete sentences using the given adverbs.

1.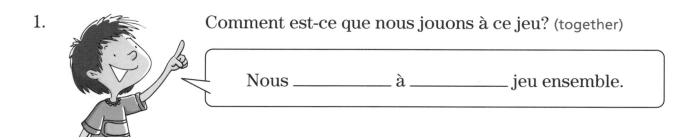

   Comment est-ce que nous jouons à ce jeu? (together)

   Nous _____ à _____ jeu ensemble.

2. Comment est-ce que tu manges? (alone)

   _____

3. Comment est-ce que le lapin saute? (quickly)

   _____

4. Comment est-ce que vous dansez? (together)

   _____

5. Comment ça va? (bad)

   _____

6. Comment est-ce que tu marches? (slowly)

   _____

7.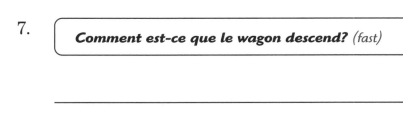

   Comment est-ce que le wagon descend? *(fast)*

   _____

L'accord du temps verbal avec l'adverbe
Time Agreement of Verbs with Adverbs

In a sentence, the adverb and the verb must always agree in time.

> **Je mange toujours mon hamburger.**
> *I'm still eating my hamburger.*

Adverbe	Verbe
• aujourd'hui • toujours • souvent	au présent e.g. Nous mangeons souvent des légumes.
• demain • lundi, vendredi, etc. + prochain • bientôt	au futur proche **aller** + infinitif e.g. Ils vont aller au parc lundi prochain.

E. Conjuguez les verbes au futur proche ou au présent selon le temps de la phrase.

Conjugate the verbs in the near future or in the present tense according to the time of the sentence.

1. Aujourd'hui, je _____ à l'école.
   <small>aller</small>

2. Samedi prochain, je _____ à l'école.
   <small>ne pas aller</small>

3. Elle _____ parfois ses légumes.
   <small>manger</small>

4. Nous _____ toujours à midi.
   <small>dîner</small>

5. Il _____ toujours!
   <small>danser</small>

6. Nous sommes fatigués mais nous _____ toujours.
   <small>nager</small>

7. Mélodie a mal à la gorge. Elle _____ visite au médecin demain.
   <small>rendre</small>

8. Ils _____ dans la cour d'école.
   <small>ne jamais jouer</small>

Expressions

En anglais : In English	En français : In French

"in _____"
    duration of time
	« dans _____ »
	    durée de temps

Unités de temps

une minute = a minute
une heure = an hour
un jour = a day
une semaine = a week
un mois = a month
un an/une année = a year
un siècle = a century

"Futur proche" is used to express events that will happen in the near future.

Always use the future tense when expressing an upcoming event with "dans".

Mélodie, j'ai besoin du téléphone!
Mélodie, I need the phone!

Je vais raccrocher dans une minute.
I am going to hang up in a minute.

F. **Complétez les réponses avec l'expression temporelle « dans » et l'unité de temps indiquée.**

Complete the answers with "dans" and the indicated unit of time.

1. Quand allez-vous finir vos devoirs? (une heure)

   Je _____ .

2. Quand vas-tu arroser ton jardin? (un jour)

   Je _____ .

3. Quand va-t-il partir? (une minute)

   Il _____ .

4. Quand prenons-nous nos vacances? (une semaine)

   Nous _____ .

La révision
- Les sports
- La vie marine
- L'impératif
- La technologie et l'Internet
- Le monde
- Au jardin
- La fête
- Quand? Où? Comment?

A. **Écrivez les mots à la bonne place et conjuguez les verbes si nécessaire.**
Write the words in the correct spaces and conjugate the verbs if necessary.

| souris | faire | cliquer | le requin | faire | arrêter |
| tuque | faire | taper | clavier | ski | nageoire | salir |

A Paul préfère les sports d'hiver. Quand il _____ du _____ , il porte toujours sa _____ .

B _____ a une grande _____ sur le dos.

C « _____ de _____ ta chemise! Il faut _____ attention! »

D Il _____ sur le _____ et il _____ avec la _____ .

un gâteau   appareil photo   Amérique du Nord   arracher
seul   tondre   Le Canada   la fête   un pays
partout   toujours   jardin

E **F** **G** **H**

E _____ est _____ en _____ .

F Pendant la fin de semaine nous travaillons dans notre _____ .

Nous _____ le gazon et nous _____ les mauvaises

herbes.

G C'est mon anniversaire! Ma mère fait _____ au chocolat pour

moi et mes amis. Nous allons faire _____ . Je vais prendre

beaucoup de photos avec mon _____ .

H Anne prend _____ son vélo _____ . Elle n'aime

pas laisser son vélo _____ .

B. Écrivez vrai ou faux.
Write true or false.

1. La pastenague a des tentacules.   _____

2. On a besoin d'un parachute pour faire du vol à voile.   _____

3. On clique sur l'icône pour ouvrir la page d'accueil.   _____

4. L'Australie est en Afrique.   _____

5. Les fleurs ne poussent jamais dans la terre.   _____

6. On joue de la musique pour s'amuser.   _____

C. Écrivez les bons mots français dans les tirets.
Write the correct French words in the blanks.

Bonjour, je m'appelle Jacques. Je suis en vacances

1._____ avec ma famille. 2._____

nous allons faire de 3._____ . Nous sommes

très 4._____ du rivage mais je n'ai pas peur

parce que je sais nager très 5._____ .

« Plongeons! » dit ma mère. Nous 6._____ du bateau dans la mer.

Sous l'eau, je 7._____ près de mon père. 8._____

parmi les 9._____ , il y a un 10._____ poisson. Je

11._____ le poisson. Il mange un bout de pain dans ma main.

12._____ il y a des poissons 13._____ ! C'est là que je

remarque des déchets partout. Il y a des fourchettes 14._____ , des

sacs de 15._____ et mêmes des 16._____ ! « Comme

c'est dangereux! ». Je 17._____ les déchets. « Je ne vais pas laisser

ça 18._____ ! C'est horrible! » . Je suis 19._____ à monter

sur le bateau. « Regardez ces déchets! » je dis à ma famille en colère. « Je ne

vais 20._____ utiliser des produits jetables à partir d'aujourd'hui! »

1. *in Mexico*	2. *today*	3. *scuba diving*	4. *far*
5. *well*	6. *to jump*	7. *to swim*	8. *there*
9. *seaweed*	10. *little*	11. *to feed*	12. *now*
13. *everywhere*	14. *disposable*	15. *chips*	16. *batteries*
17. *to take*	18. *here*	19. *the last*	20. *never*

D. Remettez le texte dans le bon ordre.
Put the events from the text in order.

1. Jacques remarque les déchets partout.
2. La famille de Jacques voyage au Mexique.
3. Jacques promet de ne jamais manger avec des produits jetables.
4. Jacques et sa famille font de la plongée sous-marine.
5. Il prend les déchets.
6. Jacques remonte sur le bateau.

_____

_____

_____

_____

_____

E. Encerclez le nom de l'objet dans l'image.
Circle the name of the object in the picture.

A  **B**   **C**   **D**

A Il prend...

le télésiège / ses skis

...au sommet de la montagne.

B La baleine / La méduse

...a des tentacules.

C On trouve le curseur sur...

le courriel / l'écran .

D Mon jeu vidéo a besoin des...

piles / ballons .

F. Écrivez la lettre dans le bon cercle.
Write the letter in the correct circle.

La voile est... ◯

L'Amérique du Nord est... ◯

Je remplis ma brouette... ◯

Dans mon jardin j'aime... ◯

On porte un gilet de sauvetage... ◯

Les étudiants bloguent... ◯

On joue à des jeux vidéo... ◯

L'Afrique est... ◯

La Corée du Sud est... ◯

Le crabe a... ◯

A avec de la terre.

B une carapace.

C au sud de l'Europe.

D pour faire du canotage.

E un sport nautique.

F pour s'amuser.

G planter des fleurs.

H à l'ouest de l'Europe.

I un pays en Asie.

J sur l'Internet.

G. Rayez l'intrus.
Cross out the word that does not belong.

1	**2**	**3**	**4**
l'écran	chanter	la planche à neige	le dauphin
la souris	réussir	l'alpinisme	la méduse
le clavier	danser	la luge	la pieuvre
le blogue	sauter	le base-ball	le calmar

5	**6**	**7**	**8**
un Japonais	la brouette	ces cadeaux	l'Irlande
un Chinois	l'herbe	ces croustilles	la France
un Mexicain	le gazon	cette boisson	l'Allemagne
un Sud-Coréen	la terre	ces hamburgers	les États-Unis

H. Reliez les termes qui s'opposent.
Link the terms that are opposites.

1. nord   •   • ouest
2. bien   •   • entendre
3. dans le ciel   •   • hier
4. parler   •   • sud
5. aujourd'hui   •   • jamais
6. est   •   • rarement
7. lentement   •   • vite
8. toujours   •   • mal
9. près   •   • loin
10. souvent   •   • à l'eau

Le magasinage

Shopping

Vocabulaire : Les magasins et leurs produits

Grammaire : Les terminaisons

Expressions : « Combien coûte... ? »

> *Combien coûte ce gros pain au chocolat?*
> How much does this big chocolate croissant cost?

A. Copiez les mots.
Copy the words.

l'épicerie
the grocery store

_____
leh·peess·ree

la caisse
the cash register

_____
lah kehs

le caissier / la caissière
the cashier

_____
luh keh·syeh
lah keh·syehr

la conserve
the canned food

_____
lah kohn·sehrv

les pâtes
the pasta

_____
leh paht

la boulangerie the bakery

_____
lah boo·laan·jree

la baguette
the baguette

_____
lah bah·get

le croissant
the croissant

_____
luh krwah·saan

le muffin
the muffin

_____
luh muh·feen

le pain
the bread

_____
luh pahn

le pain au chocolat
the chocolate croissant

_____
luh pahn oh shoh·koh·lah

le biscuit
the cookie

_____
luh beess·kwee

la tarte au citron
the lemon tart

_____
lah tahrt oh see·trohn

le dépanneur
the convenience store

_____

luh deh·pah·nuhr

le lait
the milk

_____

luh leh

la boîte de céréales
the box of cereal

_____

lah bwaht duh seh·reh·ahl

le jus
the juice

_____

luh jew

la boucherie
the butcher's shop

_____

lah boosh·ree

le poulet
the chicken

_____

luh poo·leh

le bœuf
the beef

_____

luh buhf

le porc
the pork

_____

luh pohr

la boutique
the clothing store

_____

lah boo·teek

la chemise
the shirt

_____

lah shuh·meez

le pantalon
the pants

_____

luh paan·tah·lohn

le chandail
the sweater

_____

luh shaan·dahy

B. **Écrivez le nom de l'objet et le magasin où il se trouve.**
Write the name of the object and the store where it is found.

1. _____

_____

2. _____

_____

3.  _____

_____

4. _____

_____

Les pronoms possessifs
Possessive Pronouns

possessor \ possessed	singulier		pluriel	
	masculin	**féminin**	**masculin**	**féminin**
je	**mon livre** → **le mien** my book mine	**la mienne** mine	**les miens** mine	**les miennes** mine
tu	**ton livre** → **le tien** your book yours	**la tienne** yours	**les tiens** yours	**les tiennes** yours
il/elle	**son livre** → **le sien** his/her book his/hers	**la sienne** his/hers	**les siens** his/hers	**les siennes** his/hers
nous	**notre livre** → **le nôtre** our book ours	**la nôtre** ours	**les nôtres** ours	
vous	**votre livre** → **le vôtre** your book yours	**la vôtre** yours	**les vôtres** yours	
ils/elles	**leur livre** → **le leur** their book theirs	**la leur** theirs	**les leurs** theirs	

* The gender and number of the possessive pronoun agree with the possessed object, not the possessor.

e.g.   Paul parle à **sa sœur** (f.) et Pierre parle à **la sienne** (f.).

      Paul is speaking to his sister and Pierre is speaking to his.

C.   **Remplacez l'adjectif possessif avec le bon pronom possessif.**
      Replace the possessive adjective with the correct possessive pronoun.

1.   C'est ton chien.   C'est le _____ .

2.   C'est ma tarte au citron.   _____

3.   Nous aimons notre mère.   _____

4.   Marie danse avec ses amis (m.pl.).   _____

5.   Vous allez à votre maison (f.).   _____

6.   Tu embrasses ton chat.   _____

D. Traduisez le pronom possessif en français.
Translate the possessive pronoun into French.

1.   Ce pantalon-ci est (mine) _____ .

2.   Cette tarte-là est (yours (pl.)) _____ .

3.   Ces chaussures (f.pl.) sont (theirs) _____ .

4.   Cette caisse est (ours) _____ .

5.   Ces croissants sont (hers) _____ .

6.   Ce pain au chocolat est (yours (sg.)) _____ .

E. Écrivez le bon pronom possessif.
Write the correct possessive pronoun.

1.   Je mange mon chausson.

     Mangez-vous le _____ ?
                        yours

2.   Nous allons remplir notre panier (m.).

     Vas-tu remplir _____ ?
                        yours

3.   Votre baguette est là.

     Où est _____ ?
                mine

4.   Cherches-tu ta tarte?

     Peux-tu chercher _____ aussi?
                           ours

5.   **As-tu sa chaussette?**
     Do you have her sock?

     Rends-moi ma chaussette!

     C'est _____ .
     Give me back my sock! It's mine!

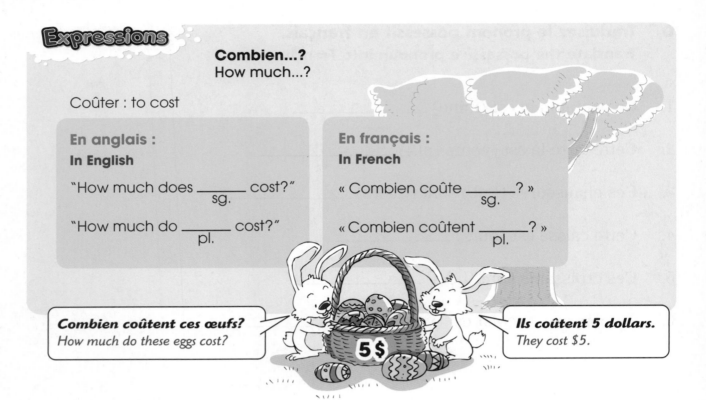

Expressions

Combien...?
How much...?

Coûter : to cost

En anglais :
In English

"How much does _____ cost?"
         sg.

"How much do _____ cost?"
         pl.

En français :
In French

« Combien coûte _____? »
            sg.

« Combien coûtent _____? »
               pl.

Combien coûtent ces œufs?
How much do these eggs cost?

5 $

Ils coûtent 5 dollars.
They cost $5.

F. **Demandez le prix et répondez à la question vous-même.**
   Ask the price and answer the question yourself.

$ = dollar(s)
e.g. 2 $ = 2 dollars

¢ = cent(s)
e.g. 15¢ = 15 cents

1. 2 $ Q : _____

        A : _____

2. 6 $ Q : _____

        A : _____

3. La conserve 70¢   Q : _____

        A : _____

4. 45¢   Q : _____

        A : _____

G. Remplissez les tirets pour demander et connaître le prix.
Fill in the blanks to ask and to learn the prices.

1.

_____ une sucette?
a lollipop

= 2 $
= 5 $

Une sucette _____ .

_____ trois sucettes?

Trois sucettes _____ .

2.

: _____ l'avion rouge?

: Il _____ .

: _____ l'avion bleu?

: Il _____ .

3.

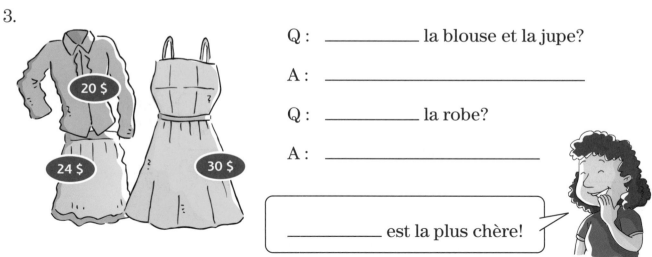

Q : _____ la blouse et la jupe?

A : _____

Q : _____ la robe?

A : _____

_____ est la plus chère!

Les verbes du 3ᵉ groupe

Verbs from the 3ʳᵈ Group

Charlie, je veux partir!
Charlie, I want to leave!

Vocabulaire : Les verbes du 3ᵉ groupe

Grammaire : La conjugaison des verbes du 3ᵉ groupe

A. **Copiez les infinitifs suivants.**
Copy the following infinitives.

« -OIR »	« -IR »	« -RE »
vouloir to want	partir to leave/depart	lire to read
voo·lwahr	*pahr·teer*	*leer*
pouvoir to be able to/can	dormir to sleep	conduire to drive
poo·vwahr	*dohr·meer*	*kohn·dweer*
devoir to have to/must	sortir to go out/to exit	écrire to write
duh·vwahr	*sohr·teer*	*eh·kreer*
savoir to know		dire to say
sah·vwahr		*deer*

J'aime sortir à vélo.
I like to get out on bike.

Parc

B. **Remplissez les tirets pour trouver l'infinitif correspondant à l'image.**
Fill in the blanks to find the infinitive corresponding to the picture.

A Anne aime __ __ __ __ __ __ avec son ours.

B Andrée peut __ __ __ __ le français.

C Les enfants aiment __ __ __ __ les réponses.

D Daniel et Caroline vont __ __ __ __ __ __ __ dans leurs journaux.

E Ils aiment __ __ __ __ __ __ en vacances.

F Le chien ne veut pas __ __ __ __ __ __ de la maison. Il veut regarder un film.

 Grammaire

« -OIR » : pouvoir, savoir, devoir et vouloir

"Pouvoir" and "vouloir" are conjugated in the same way. However, "savoir" and "devoir" are completely irregular.

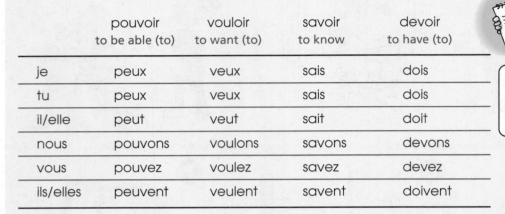

	pouvoir to be able (to)	vouloir to want (to)	savoir to know	devoir to have (to)
je	peux	veux	sais	dois
tu	peux	veux	sais	dois
il/elle	peut	veut	sait	doit
nous	pouvons	voulons	savons	devons
vous	pouvez	voulez	savez	devez
ils/elles	peuvent	veulent	savent	doivent

All four of these verbs can be followed by an infinitive.

e.g.
- Je peux **marcher**.
  I can walk.
- Je veux **manger**.
  I want to eat.
- Je sais **nager**.
  I know how to swim.
- Je dois **manger**.
  I have to eat.

C. **Encerclez ou écrivez la bonne forme du verbe.**
Circle or write the correct form of the verb.

1. Marie   veux voulons veut   manger le petit déjeuner.

2. Marc et moi   sais savez savons   chercher de les réponses.

3. Il ne   dois doit devez   pas aller à l'école aujourd'hui.

4. Il _____ (must) savoir la leçon.

5. _____ (can) -vous voir l'écran?

6. Je _____ (must) accepter tes suggestions.

7. Marc et toi _____ (must) avoir de la chance!
   have good luck

« -IR » irregular : dormir, partir et sortir

These irregular « -IR » verbs from the 3rd group are all conjugated in the same way.

	dormir to sleep	partir to leave	sortir to get out
	dorm~~ir~~	part~~ir~~	sort~~ir~~
je	dor**s**	par**s**	sor**s**
tu	dor**s**	par**s**	sor**s**
il/elle	dor**t**	par**t**	sor**t**
	dorm~~ir~~	part~~ir~~	sort~~ir~~
nous	dorm**ons**	part**ons**	sort**ons**
vous	dorm**ez**	part**ez**	sort**ez**
ils/elles	dorm**ent**	part**ent**	sort**ent**

> **Nous dormons au soleil pour nous faire bronzer.**
> *We're sleeping in the sun to get a tan.*

D. Écrivez la bonne forme du verbe.
Write the correct form of the verb.

Rémi et son frère Olivier _____ ensemble dans leur chambre à
dormir

coucher. Les draps₁ jaunes _____ sur le lit de Rémi et les draps
être

verts _____ son sur le lit d'Olivier. Les matins, leur mère crie :
être

« _____ du lit! Vous _____ trop! » Elle ouvre les rideaux
sortir   dormir

et les garçons ne _____ plus _____ . « Allez! » dit Olivier,
pouvoir   dormir

« _____ du lit Rémi! » « _____-nous _____
sortir   devoir   partir

si tôt? » demande Rémi. Et cela se répète chaque jour...

---

1. *le drap : bed sheet*

Grammaire

« -RE » irregular : dire, lire, écrire et conduire

	dire to say	lire to read	écrire to write	conduire to drive
je	dis	lis	écris	conduis
tu	dis	lis	écris	conduis
il/elle	dit	lit	écrit	conduit
nous	disons	lisons	écrivons	conduisons
vous	dites	lisez	écrivez	conduisez
ils/elles	disent	lisent	écrivent	conduisent

Je conduis ma voiture.
I'm driving my car.

E. **Écrivez la bonne forme du verbe.**
Write the correct form of the verb.

1. —— lire——

il _____

nous _____

2. —— dire——

tu _____

elle _____

3. — conduire —

elle _____

vous _____

4. —— écrire ——

tu _____

j' _____

5. —— lire ——

vous _____

tu _____

6. —— dire——

ils _____

nous _____

7. Nous _____ (écrire) des cartes de Noël chaque année.

8. Faites attention quand vous _____ (conduire).

9. Je _____ (lire) et j' _____ (écrire) en français.

10. Qu'est-ce que vous _____ (dire)?

F. **Écrivez l'infinitif des verbes soulignés, ainsi que la personne et le nombre auxquels les verbes sont conjugués.**
Write the infinitive form of the underlined verbs as well as the person and number to which they are conjugated.

C'est le weekend! Moi et mes sœurs <u>voulons</u> jouer au parc, mais nous <u>devons</u> d'abord nettoyer nos chambres. « <u>Dors</u>-tu encore, Claire? » je demande.

« Je <u>sais</u> qu'elle ne <u>dort</u> plus! » crie ma sœur, Mélodie. « Regarde! Ses yeux sont ouverts! »

nombre / personne	singulier	pluriel
1re	Je	Nous
2^e	Tu	Vous
3^e	Il/Elle	Ils/Elles

Claire disparaît sous les draps, « Laissez-moi tranquille! Je <u>veux</u> dormir », dit-elle. « Si tu <u>pars</u> pour le parc avec nous, tu <u>dois</u> sortir du lit maintenant! » je dis. « C'est Maman qui nous <u>conduit</u> aujourd'hui. » « Je m'en fiche! <u>Partez</u> sans moi! » répond Claire et elle retourne au lit.

1. __vouloir__ , __1^{re}__ , __pluriel__   2. _____ , ____ , _____

3. _____ , ____ , _____   4. _____ , ____ , _____

5. _____ , ____ , _____   6. _____ , ____ , _____

7. _____ , ____ , _____   8. _____ , ____ , _____

9. _____ , ____ , _____   10. _____ , ____ , _____

Le journal

The Newspaper

> **Je vais chercher un nouveau chien dans les petites annonces.**
> I'm going to search in the classifieds for a new dog.

Vocabulaire : Le journal et les nouvelles

Grammaire : Le futur proche

A. Copiez les mots.
Copy the words.

le journal
the newspaper

luh joor·nahl

les médias
the media

leh meh·dyah

l'information (f.)
the information

lahn·fohr·mah·syohn

le gros titre
the headline

luh groh teetr

le sous-titre
the subtitle

luh soo·teetr

la météo
the weather forecast

lah meh·teh·oh

la chronique
the newspaper column

lah kroh·neek

Monde
World

mohnd

Voyages
Travel

vwah·yahj

Emploi
Employment

aam·plwah

Culture
Culture

kewl·twer

Cinéma
Movies

see·neh·mah

Sports
Sports

spohr

Dessins
Cartoons

deh·sahn

Économie
Economy

eh·koh·noh·mee

Société
Society

soh·syeh·teh

Loisirs
Entertainment

lwah·zeer

Petites Annonces
Classifieds

puh·teet zah·nohns

Politique
Politics

poh·lee·teek

B. **Lisez les gros titres et écrivez le nom de la section où ils se trouvent.**
Read the headlines and write the names of the newspaper sections to which they belong.

A Japon : dans la vallée perdue.

B *La saison des pluies!*

C Nouveau film de Mme Marin – fantastique!

D « Un coup d'état d'un genre nouveau »

E L'équipe canadienne de hockey gagne deux médailles d'or!

F *Chat perdu* (Récompense)
Contactez Julie à julie@popmail.com.

A _____

B _____

C _____

D _____

E _____

F _____

C. **Reliez les phrases aux bons mots.**
Match the sentences with the correct words.

1. Des informations politiques se trouvent dans... •

2. Le sous-titre est moins visible que... •

3. Les articles d'un journal sont divisés en... •

4. La météo nous donne des informations sur... •

5. Un journaliste écrit des articles dans... •

• chroniques.

• la température.

• la section « Politique » .

• un journal.

• le gros titre.

Le futur proche
Immediate Future

Futur proche (ALLER + infinitif)

- is formed with the present tense of ALLER and an infinitive verb

- is used to express an action that will happen in the near future, and is linked to a situation happening in the present

ALLER + LIRE		
je	**vais**	lire
tu	**vas**	lire
il/elle	**va**	lire
nous	**allons**	lire
vous	**allez**	lire
ils/elles	**vont**	lire

Est-ce que tu vas jouer avec moi?
Are you going to play with me?

D. Récrivez les phrases au futur proche.
Rewrite the sentences in "futur proche".

1. La section « Société » annonce une grève.

   _____

2. Nous lisons la section « Météo » pour vérifier la température.

   _____

3. Monsieur le Premier ministre part en France.

   _____

4. Mon père veut la section « Sports ».

   _____

5. Marie lit le journal chaque jour.

   _____

6. Le journaliste écrit un article sur la grève.

   _____

E. Construisez des phrases au futur proche avec les mots donnés.
Make sentences in "futur proche" with the given words.

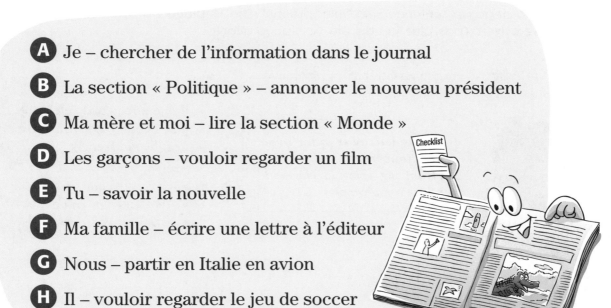

A Je – chercher de l'information dans le journal

B La section « Politique » – annoncer le nouveau président

C Ma mère et moi – lire la section « Monde »

D Les garçons – vouloir regarder un film

E Tu – savoir la nouvelle

F Ma famille – écrire une lettre à l'éditeur

G Nous – partir en Italie en avion

H Il – vouloir regarder le jeu de soccer

A Je _____ chercher de l'information dans _____ .

B _____

C _____

D _____

E _____

F _____

G _____

H _____

Le futur proche au négatif
Immediate Future in the Negative

To form a negative sentence with "futur proche", "ne" is placed before "aller" and the negative adverb (pas, plus, jamais, etc.) is placed after it.

ne + aller + negative adverb + infinitive

Je ne vais plus jouer avec ces jouets!
I am not going to play with these toys anymore!

Remember, two elements are needed to form the negative in French.

- ne...pas *not*
- ne...plus *no more*
- ne...jamais *never*

F. Mettez les phrases au négatif.
Make the positive sentences negative.

1. Il va lire la section « Société ». (ne...pas)

   _____

2. Mes fleurs vont toujours vouloir de l'eau. (ne...jamais)

   _____

3. Claudette et Thérèse vont pouvoir regarder un film. (ne...plus)

   _____

4. Je vais aller au magasin à pied. (ne...pas)

   _____

5. Zoé va écrire une lettre à ses parents. (ne...pas)

   _____

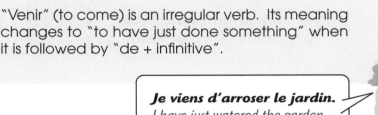

Expressions

Le passé récent
Recent Past

En anglais :
In English
"to have just done something"

En français :
In French
« venir de + infinitif »

singulier

je vien**s**
tu vien**s**
il/elle vien**t**

pluriel

nous ven**ons**
vous ven**ez**
ils/elles vien**nent**

"Venir" (to come) is an irregular verb. Its meaning changes to "to have just done something" when it is followed by "de + infinitive".

Je viens d'arroser le jardin.
I have just watered the garden.

G. **Écrivez « P » à côté des phrases au passé et « F » à côté de celles au futur.**
Write "P" beside sentences in the past and "F" beside those in the future.

1. Elle vient de remplir le bol. _____

2. Nous allons lire le journal. _____

3. Pierre et Julie vont manger au restaurant. _____

4. Je viens de finir mon travail. _____

5. Tu vas porter ta robe noire. _____

6. Marie vient de m'écrire une longue lettre. _____

7. Ils viennent de répondre au téléphone. _____

8. Je vais toujours aimer mon chat. _____

Les nombres : de 1 à 1000

Numbers: 1 to 1000

Vocabulaire : Les nombres de 1 à 1000

Révision : Les expressions de quantité

Cette bague coûte neuf cent dollars.
That ring costs $900.

Je n'ai pas assez d'argent.
I don't have enough money.

A. Copiez les mots.
Copy the words.

cent   **100**

saan

cent dix   **110**

saan deess

deux cents   **200**

duh saan

deux cent vingt   **220**

duh saan vahn

trois cents   **300**

trwah saan

trois cent trente   **330**

trwah saan traant

quatre cents   **400**

kahtr saan

quatre cent quarante   **440**

kahtr saan kah·raant

cinq cents   **500**

sahnk saan

cinq cent cinquante   **550**

sank saan sahn·kaant

six cents   **600**

seess saan

six cent soixante   **660**

seess saan swah·saant

sept cents   **700**

seht saan

sept cent soixante-dix   **770**

seht saan swah·saant deess

huit cents   800   huit cent quatre-vingts   880

weet saan   *weet saan kah·truh·vahn*

neuf cents   900   neuf cent quatre-vingt-dix   990

nuhf saan   *nuhf saan kah·truh·vahn·deess*

mille   1000   1001 $

_____ dollars

meel   *meel eh euhn*

B. Écrivez les nombres en lettres ou en chiffres.
Write the numbers in words or in digits.

1. 347 _____ cent quarante-_____

2. 892 huit _____ quatre-vingt-_____

3. 116 cent _____

4. 664 _____ cent _____-_____

5. 501 _____ _____ un

6. 755 sept cent _____-_____

7. deux cent soixante-treize

8. quatre cent trente-quatre

9. sept cent dix-huit

10. cinq cent cinquante-cinq

11. trois cent douze

C. Écrivez le prix de chaque objet en lettres.
Write the price of each item in words.

Ça coûte...

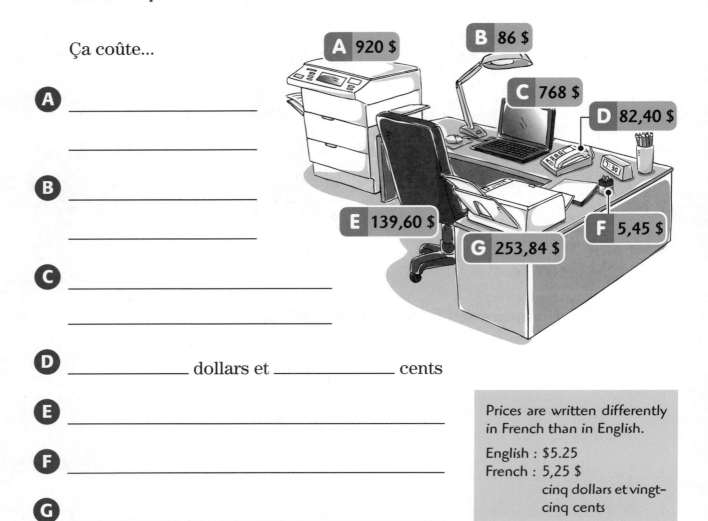

A _____

_____

B _____

_____

C _____

_____

D _____ dollars et _____ cents

E _____

F _____

G _____

> Prices are written differently in French than in English.
>
> English : $5.25
> French : 5,25 $
> cinq dollars et vingt-cinq cents

D. Faites les calculs et écrivez les réponses en lettres.
Do the calculations and write the answers in words.

1. Sept plus sept cent soixante-dix égalent _____ .

2. Mille moins trois cent quarante égalent _____ .

3. Quatre cents plus quatre-vingt-dix-sept égalent _____ .

4. Deux cents plus sept cents quatorze égalent _____ .

Expressions

En anglais :

In English
- x times y makes xy
- x over y makes $\frac{x}{y}$

En français :

In French
- x fois y, ça fait xy
- x sur y, ça fait $\frac{x}{y}$

$12 \times 6 = 72$

12 fois 6, ça fait 72. 72 personnes peuvent s'attabler autour de 12 tables.

12 times 6 makes 72. 72 people can be seated around 12 tables.

E. **Trouvez la réponse. Ensuite écrivez l'équation en lettres.**

Find the answer. Then write the equation in words.

A $1000 \div 4 = $ _____

B $2 \times 347 = $ _____

C $260 \times 3 = $ _____

D $\dfrac{550}{5} = $ _____

E $\dfrac{612}{6} = $ _____

F $10 \times 82 = $ _____

L'équation en lettres

A _____

B _____

C _____

D _____

E _____

F _____

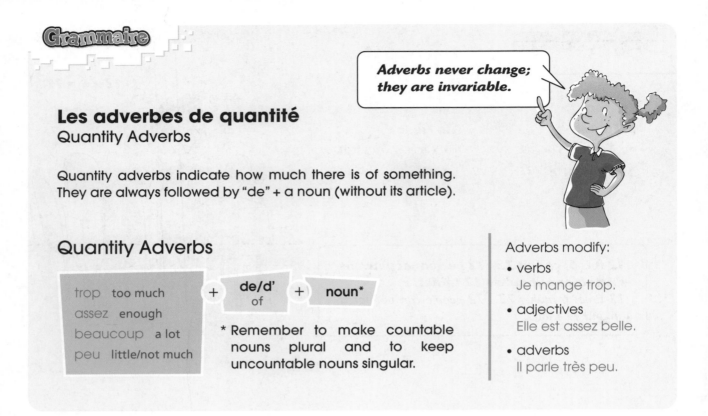

Les adverbes de quantité
Quantity Adverbs

Quantity adverbs indicate how much there is of something. They are always followed by "de" + a noun (without its article).

Adverbs never change; they are invariable.

Quantity Adverbs

trop	too much
assez	enough
beaucoup	a lot
peu	little/not much

+ de/d' of **+** noun*

* Remember to make countable nouns plural and to keep uncountable nouns singular.

Adverbs modify:
- verbs
  Je mange trop.
- adjectives
  Elle est assez belle.
- adverbs
  Il parle très peu.

F. **Récrivez les phrases avec les adverbes de quantité donnés.**
Rewrite the sentences with the quantity adverbs given.

1. Jean et Marie ont des enfants. (assez de)

   _____

2. En hiver, il y a de la neige. (trop de)

   _____

3. Les fleurs poussent dans son jardin. (beaucoup de)

   _____

4. Il a de l'argent pour acheter la bague. (peu de)

   _____

5. Elle boit de la boisson gazeuse. (beaucoup de)

   _____

G. **Faites les problèmes et écrivez les réponses en lettres.**
Solve the problems and write the answers in words.

1. Mon père a 41 ans, ma mère a 4 ans moins que mon père. Quel âge a ma mère?

    _____

2. Béatrice possède₁ cent quinze livres. Annie et son frère en ont deux fois plus, Bernard en a cinq fois moins.

    a. Combien de livres ont Annie et son frère?

        _____

    b. Combien de livres a Bernard?

        _____

3. Samuel veut faire un gâteau. La recette lui dit de mettre trois cents grammes de farine₂ pour six personnes. Samuel veut un gâteau pour seulement₃ deux personnes. Combien de grammes de farine doit-il y mettre?

    _____

4. Un mètre est cent centimètres, donc un centimètre est _____ sur _____ d'un mètre.

5. Un mètre est mille millimètres, donc un millimètre est _____ sur _____ d'un mètre.

    1. *posséder* : to possess, to own   2. *grammes de farine* : grams of flour
    3. *seulement* : only

Au musée

At the Museum

Vocabulaire : Les objets au musée

Grammaire : Les doubles constructions

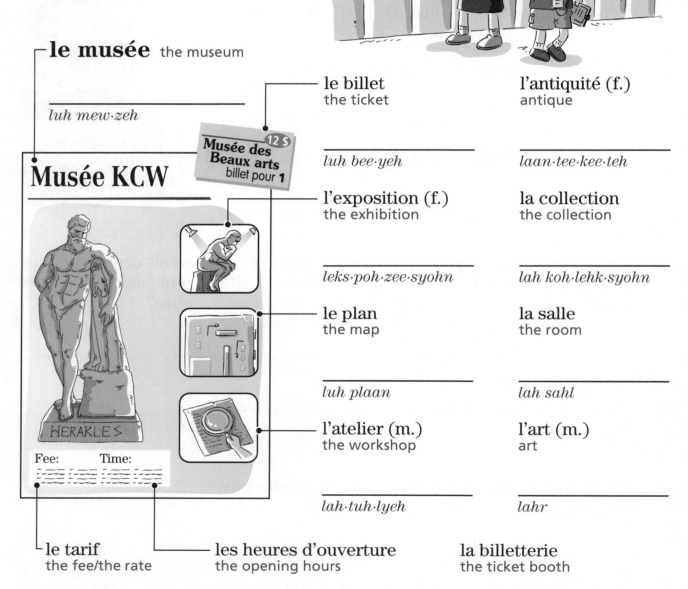

> **Je ne veux pas passer la journée ici!**
> I don't want to spend the day here!

A. Copiez les mots.
Copy the words.

le musée the museum

luh mew·zeh

Musée KCW

Musée des Beaux arts
billet pour **1**
12 $

HERAKLES

Fee: Time:

le tarif
the fee/the rate

luh tah·reef

le billet
the ticket

luh bee·yeh

l'exposition (f.)
the exhibition

leks·poh·zee·syohn

le plan
the map

luh plaan

l'atelier (m.)
the workshop

lah·tuh·lyeh

les heures d'ouverture
the opening hours

leh zuhr doo·vehr·tewr

l'antiquité (f.)
antique

laan·tee·kee·teh

la collection
the collection

lah koh·lehk·syohn

la salle
the room

lah sahl

l'art (m.)
art

lahr

la billetterie
the ticket booth

lah bee·yeh·tree

Les œuvres du musée sont...
The works at the museum are...

historique historic

_____

eess·toh·reek

precious/valuable

précieux   **précieuse**

_____   _____

preh·syuh   *preh·syuhz*

old

vieux   **vieille**

_____   _____

vyuh   *vyehy*

ancient

ancien   **ancienne**

_____   _____

aan·syahn   *aan·syehn*

fascinating

fascinant   **fascinante**

_____   _____

fah·see·naan   *fah·see·naant*

delicate

délicat   **délicate**

_____   _____

deh·lee·kah   *deh·lee·kaht*

Au musée on peut...
At the museum we can...

observer to observe

_____

ohb·zehr·veh

toucher to touch

_____

too·sheh

remarquer to notice

_____

ruh·mahr·keh

passer* to spend time/to pass

_____

pah·seh

exposer to exhibit/to display

_____

ehks·poh·zeh

guider to guide

_____

gee·deh

visiter to visit

_____

vee·zee·teh

Find the verb "passer" in your own French-English dictionary and compare it to the one below.

la prononciation ─┐   ┌─ verbe intransitif
                           (doesn't take an object)

┌─ verbe transitif (takes an object)

l'entrée du ──• **passer** (pase) **vi 1** : to pass, to go, to
dictionnaire   come past. e.g. Le train va bientôt
                passer. *The train will be coming past
                soon.*

vt 2 : to cross, to go through e.g. Je passe
la rivière à la nage. *I swim across the river.*

3 : to spend (time) e.g. passer sa vie : *to
spend one's life* e.g. passer une heure/
une minute/du temps : *to spend an hour/a
minute/some time*

passer sur ──• ~ sur – to pass over, to overlook e.g. Je
(repeat the   veux bien passer sur cette erreur. *I'm
entry)   willing to overlook this mistake.*

B. Remplissez les tirets avec les bons mots.
Fill in the blanks with the correct words.

Christophe vient de 1._____ une salle

2._____ . La salle 3._____ une collection

4._____ . Il 5._____ les antiquités mais

il y a une affiche qui dit : « Ne touchez pas! » Il regarde bien

6._____ . Il aime bien visiter 7._____

près de 8._____ des pierres* 9._____ .

1. to notice
2. fascinating
3. to display
4. historic
5. to want to touch
6. the map
7. the workshop
8. the exhibition
9. valuable

> * Look up the word "pierre" in your French-English dictionary to find its gender before writing the corresponding adjective.
> (nm = nom masculin, nf = nom féminin)

C. Trouvez le mot « toucher » dans votre dictionnaire. Ensuite répondez aux questions.
Find the word "toucher" in your dictionary. Then answer the questions.

1. How many entries are there for the word "toucher"? _____

2. What are the grammatical roles of the first entry and the second entry?
(grammatical role: verb, noun, adjective, adverb, etc.) Write the meanings of "toucher".

toucher$_1$: _____   toucher$_2$: _____

meaning : _____   meaning : _____

_____   _____

_____   _____

Les doubles constructions
Double Verb Constructions

Double verb constructions have a conjugated auxiliary verb followed by an infinitive.

Auxiliary Verbs	pouvoir	Je peux arroser les plantes. I can water the plants.
	vouloir	Nous voulons manger de la pizza. We want to eat some pizza.
	savoir	Il sait parler français. He knows how to speak French.
	devoir	Vous devez lire l'unité 10 pour les conjugaisons. You must read unit 10 for the conjugations.

D. Remplissez les tirets avec la bonne forme du verbe.
Fill in the blanks with the correct form of the verbs.

1. Le public _____ cette œuvre.

pouvoir toucher

2. Moi et mon chien _____ dehors.

devoir attendre

3. Je _____ les visiteurs vers les nouvelles collections.

pouvoir guider

4. Ils _____ le musée demain.

vouloir visiter

5. Tu _____ une heure dans chaque salle.

devoir passer

6. Vous _____ des œuvres canadiennes.

pouvoir regarder

7. Je _____ les heures d'ouverture.

vouloir savoir

8. Ils _____ les œuvres anciennes.

savoir garder

Expressions

"Devoir" and "pouvoir" are auxiliary verbs that can be used to give commands, suggestions, or advice in a more polite manner, in comparison to those given with the imperative.

Imperative (giving an order) : e.g. Mangez vos légumes!   Eat your vegetables!

devoir + infinitive :

(giving a polite suggestion)

> ***Vous devez manger vos légumes.***
> *You have to eat your vegetables.*

pouvoir + infinitive :

(asking a question politely)

e.g.   Pouvez-vous manger vos légumes?
       Can/Could you eat your vegetables?

(making a polite suggestion)

e.g.   Vous pouvez dormir plus tôt.
       You could sleep earlier.

E.   Demandez un service poliment en utilisant « pouvoir ».
   Ask a favour politely using "pouvoir".

1.   Vous devez aller à la classe de musique.

   _____-vous _____ à la classe de musique?

2.   Il doit faire ses devoirs.

   _____

3.   Tu dois marcher plus vite.

   _____

4.   Nous devons téléphoner à Marie.

   _____

5.   Vous devez attendre mon frère.

   _____

F. Remplissez les tirets. Ensuite relisez la brochure et répondez aux questions.
Fill in the blanks. Then reread the brochure and answer the questions.

_____ principale :
the room

_____ des œuvres d'Emily Carr
the exhibition

_____ : 9 h à 18 h
the opening hours

Musée des beaux arts
Museum of Fine Arts

Le musée des beaux arts _____ les _____ d'Emily Carr
                        is going to exhibit   art works

en août. Vous _____ ses peintures de près₁ et vous _____
               could/may observe   could/may visit

sa maison en regardant₂ la projection du film "Emily Carr : la vie d'une artiste".

Vous _____ acheter vos _____ en avance₃. Il y a des guides
     must   tickets

qui _____ les visiteurs. _____-nous en groupes₄!
    could/can guide   visiter (impératif)

| 1. | de près : up close | 2. | en regardant : by watching |
| 3. | en avance : in advance | 4. | en groupes : in groups |

1. Où est-ce qu'on peut voir les œuvres d'Emily Carr? C'est quel mois?

    _____

2. Qu'est-ce qu'on peut observer de près?

    _____

3. Est-ce qu'on peut visiter sa maison de près?

    _____

4. Quand est-ce qu'on doit acheter les billets?

    _____

Les médias

The Media

Vocabulaire : Les moyens de communication

Grammaire : Les constructions « verbe + infinitif »

- au négatif
- à l'interrogatif

La presse écrite

Pardon monsieur, la télévision n'est pas de la presse écrite!
Sorry, Sir, television is not print media!

A. Copiez les mots.
Copy the words.

les médias
the media

_____
leh meh·dyah

la presse écrite
the print media

_____
lah prehs eh·kreet

la radio
the radio

_____
lah rah·dyoh

la télévision
the television

_____
lah teh·leh·vee·zyohn

le réseau
the network

_____
luh reh·zoh

le public
the public

_____
luh pew·bleek

l'Internet
the Internet

_____
lahn·tehr·neht

le journal
the newspaper

_____
luh joor·nahl

a reader ━━━━━
un lecteur

_____
euhn lehk·tuhr

une lectrice

_____
ewn lehk·treess

a viewer ━━━━━
un spectateur

_____
euhn spehk·tah·tuhr

une spectatrice

_____
ewn spehk·tah·treess

a writer ━━━━━
un écrivain

_____
euhn eh·kree·vahn

une écrivaine

_____
ewn eh·kree·vehn

a listener ━━━━━
un auditeur

_____
euhn oh·dee·tuhr

une auditrice

_____
ewn oh·dee·treess

a broadcaster ━━━━━
une personnalité de la radio/télévision

_____
ewn pehr·soh·nah·lee·teh

avouer (à)
to admit/to confess (to)

annoncer (à)
to announce/to report (to)

_____

_____

ah·voo·eh

ah·nohn·seh

téléviser
to broadcast on TV

diffuser
to broadcast on the radio

Like "manger, nager, and télécharger", "annoncer" takes an irregular ending in the 1st person plural.

sg.	pl.
j'annonce	nous annonçons
tu annonces	vous annoncez
il/elle annonce	ils/elles annoncent

_____

_____

teh·leh·vee·zeh

dee·few·zeh

communiquer (à)
to communicate (to)

mettre à jour
to update

_____

_____

koh·mew·nee·keh

mehtr ah jour

connecter (à)
to connect (to)

déclarer (à)
to declare (to)

_____

_____

koh·nehk·teh

deh·klah·reh

B. Associez les deux parties pour faire une phrase.
Link the two parts to form a sentence.

1. Un écrivain écrit pour...   •   • la radio.

2. On peut entendre les émissions à... •   • la télévision.

3. L'Internet est un très grand...   •   • presse écrite.

4. Un spectateur est celui qui regarde... •   • informations.

5. Le journal est une forme de...   •   • ses lecteurs.

6. Les médias communiquent des...   •   • réseau.

Les doubles constructions
Double Verb Constructions

Double verb constructions have one conjugated auxiliary verb followed by an infinitive verb.

Remember, in double verb constructions, the auxiliary verb and the infinitive verb have the same subject.

e.g.   **Je** veux parler à Marie.
       "Je" is the subject of "veux" and "parler".

Double Verb Construction	
conjugated auxiliary verb	+ infinitive

The infinitive often directly follows verbs that express:

- an obligation or ability:

  devoir (to have to),
  pouvoir (to be able to),
  savoir (to know), etc.

- an opinion or a declaration:

  vouloir (to want), déclarer (to declare),
  annoncer (to announce), penser (to think/consider),
  avouer (to admit), aimer (to like), etc.

e.g.   Paul avoue être fort.
       Paul admits that he is strong.

C.   Transformez les phrases en constructions doubles.
Change the sentences into double verb constructions.

1. Je vais à l'école à pied. (devoir)

   _____

2. La CBC est un réseau national. (déclarer)

   _____

3. Vous écrivez aux écrivains de cet article. (vouloir)

   _____

4. Ils parlent à leurs parents. (penser)

   _____

Les doubles constructions et l'inversion
Double Verb Constructions and Inversion

Changing sentences with double verb constructions into questions using inversion is done in the same way as with sentences that have a single verb. The conjugated auxiliary verb exchanges place with the subject. The infinitive remains in its place.

e.g. Samuel veut aller à l'école.

Veut-il aller à l'école?
Does he want to go to school?

Marie aime jouer.

Aime-t-elle jouer?
* If the verb ends in a vowel, insert "t".
Does she like to play?

D. **Transformez les phrases en questions avec l'inversion.**
Change the sentences into questions using inversion.

1. Marie pense être une bonne auditrice.

   _____

2. L'Internet peut connecter les gens.

   _____

3. Tu entends parler les vieilles dames.

   _____

4. Le public aime regarder les comédies de situation à la télévision.

   _____

5. Tu dois prendre le métro aujourd'hui.

   _____

6. Nous allons manger des pommes de terre.

   _____

7. Ils avouent être les amis de Paul.

   _____

The negative adverbs "ne" and "pas/jamais/plus, etc." go before and after the conjugated verb respectively. The infinitive verb follows.

e.g. Je veux manger du gâteau.

Je ne veux pas manger du gâteau.

I don't want to eat cake.

ne + conjugated auxiliary verb + pas plus jamais guère + infinitive

E. Mettez les phrases au négatif.
Make the positive sentences negative.

1. Nous devons avoir honte. (ne...pas)

    _____

2. Joseph et Sarah veulent annoncer la nouvelle. (ne...plus)

    _____

3. Qui est-ce qui pense être beau? (ne...jamais)

    _____

4. Tu peux communiquer avec tes parents sur l'Internet. (ne...guère)

    _____

F. Cochez la phrase qui correspond à l'image.
Check the sentence that matches the picture.

1.

Ⓐ Elle pense pouvoir voler.

Ⓑ Elle peut voler.

2.

Ⓐ Elle avoue avoir peur.

Ⓑ Elle n'a pas peur.

G. Remplissez les tirets pour compléter l'article.
Fill in the blanks to complete the article.

Peut-être₁ un jour...
Maybe one day...

_____-vous que le premier
<u>savoir</u>

ordinateur remonte à₂ 1946? Il pèse₃ 30 tonnes et

il _____ une maison de dimension
<u>pouvoir remplir</u>

normale. Aujourd'hui je _____ que les gens _____
<u>devoir avouer</u> <u>pouvoir se connecter</u>

aux réseaux internationaux à n'importe quel₄ moment du jour. Les ordinateurs

de nos jours pèsent beaucoup moins et on dit que l'Internet _____
<u>aller remplacer</u>

la presse écrite. Est-ce que cela _____
<u>vouloir dire</u>

que nous _____ un jour assister₅ aux
<u>pouvoir</u>

écoles virtuelles₆?

1. *peut-être : maybe*
2. *remonter à : date back to*
3. *peser : to weigh*
4. *n'importe quel : no matter which, regardless*
5. *assister à : to attend*
6. *virtuel(le) : virtual*

H. Relisez l'article et répondez aux questions.
Read the article again and answer the questions.

1. Combien pèse le premier ordinateur? _____

2. Qu'est-ce qui peut remplacer la presse écrite? _____

3. Est-ce que vous pouvez trouver un autre titre (title) pour cet article?

_____

Le transport

Transportation

Vocabulaire : Les moyens de transport

Grammaire : Les prépositions « à » et « de »

> *Je vais à l'école à vélo, parce que je suis en retard.*
> I'm going to school by bike because I'm late.

A. Copiez les mots.
Copy the words.

aller à...
to go by

pied

_____
pyeh

cheval

_____
shuh·vahl

vélo

_____
veh·loh

aller en...
to go by

 train

_____
trahn

 avion

_____
ah·vee·yohn

 autobus

_____
oh·toh·bews

bateau

_____
bah·toh

 métro

_____
meh·troh

les rails **the tracks/rails**

_____
leh rahy

le pilote **the pilot**

_____
luh pee·loht

l'arrêt **the stop**

_____
lah·reh

la voile **the sail**

_____
lah vwahl

le billet **the ticket**

_____
luh bee·yeh

B. **Associez les phrases incomplètes aux bons mots.**
Match the incomplete sentences with the correct words.

1. Le train va sur... •   • un avion.

2. J'attends l'autobus à... •   • une voile.

3. Le bateau de Louise a... •   • l'arrêt d'autobus.

4. Le pilote conduit... •   • les rails.

C. **Décrivez comment les personnages arrivent à leurs destinations avec le verbe « aller ». Utilisez la bonne préposition.**
Describe how the characters will arrive at their destinations using the correct form of the verb "aller". Use the correct preposition.

A Je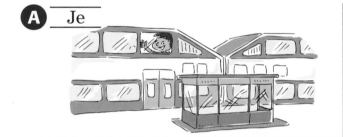

B Tu

C Nous

D Ils

E Elle

A Je _____ en _____ .

B _____

C _____

D _____

E _____

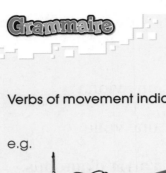

Grammaire

« À » et « de »
"To" and "From"

Verbs of movement indicate displacement "from" one place "to" another.

e.g.

Paris

Toronto

Je vais **de** Toronto **à** Paris en avion.
I fly from Toronto to Paris.

Verbs of Movement:

aller (de/à)	to go (from/to)
arriver (de/à)	to arrive (from/to)
descendre (de/à)	to go/come down (from/to)
monter (de/à)	to come/go up (from/to)
sortir (de/à)	to go out/exit (from/to)
venir (de/à)	to come (from/to)

D. Décrivez les mouvements dans les images.
Describe the movements in the picture.

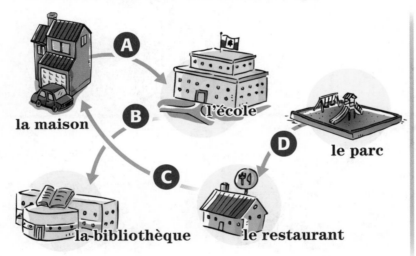

la maison · l'école · le parc · la bibliothèque · le restaurant

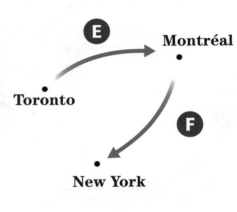

Montréal · Toronto · New York

A (Je/arriver) J'arrive _____ la maison à _____ .

B (Nous/descendre) _____

C (Tu/monter) _____

D (Elle/aller) _____

E (Je/revenir) _____

F (Vous/arriver) _____

E. **Utilisez la bonne forme du verbe « venir de » pour indiquer le pays d'où ils viennent.**

Use the correct form of the verb "venir de" to indicate where each person is from.

1. les États-Unis

   Tu _____ des États-Unis.

« **venir** » *to come*	
singulier	**pluriel**
je viens	nous venons
tu viens	vous venez
il/elle vient	ils/elles viennent

2.
   le Canada

   Je _____
   _____

3. le Maroc

   a. Marie et Julie _____

   b. Karim _____

4. la France

   a. Nous _____

   b. Elle _____

5.
   l'Angleterre

   a. Vous _____

   b. Ils _____

F. **Remplissez les tirets avec la bonne préposition « de / à ».**

Fill in the blanks with the correct preposition "de / à".

1. J'arrive _____ la maison _____ l'école à 8 h 30.

2. Je reviens _____ la maison _____ l'école à 15 h 30.

3. Tu descends _____ la bibliothèque chaque jour.

4. Nous allons _____ la cour d'école pour jouer.

Verbes suivis de « à/de »
Verbs followed by "à/de"

"À" and "de" can also come after a number of verbs that do not indicate movement but which have a "destination" or "point of reference".

à to
- parler à   to talk to
- donner à   to give to
- répondre à   to answer to
- dire à   to tell/say to

e.g.   Je dis mes secrets à mon ami.
       I tell my secrets to my friend.

de from/about
- parler de   to talk about
- rêver de   to dream about
- profiter de   to make the most of
- avoir besoin de   to be in need of

e.g.   Nous rêvons des cadeaux.
       We dream about gifts.

G. **Remplissez les tirets avec la bonne préposition.**
Fill in the blanks with the correct prepositions.

1.   Je rêve parfois _____ mes cousins.

2.   Vous penser _____ vos enfants.

3.   Ils profitent toujours _____ l'occasion.

4.   Lucie a besoin _____ une dentiste.

5.   Nous donnons des cadeaux _____ nos amis à Noël.

6.   Répondez _____ la question.

7.   Elle parle _____ son chat _____ ses amis.

8.   Je dis _____ ma mère de me faire un gâteau.

H. **Remplissez les tirets avec la bonne préposition et répondez aux questions.**
Fill in the blanks with the correct prepositions and answer the questions.

Alice et ses parents viennent d'arriver _____ Paris _____ avion. Ils rentrent _____ l'aéroport _____ leur hôtel _____ 4 h. Ils vont tout de suite₁ _____ lit pour pouvoir se réveiller₂ à l'heure du déjeuner. Alice s'endort₃ vite et elle rêve _____ croissants, _____ pains au chocolat et _____ tartes aux abricots. Le matin, elle se réveille à 7 h, va _____ la salle de bain prendre une douche, sort _____ sa chambre, et descend _____ restaurant avec sa mère. Quand elle arrive _____ restaurant, elle ne voit personne. La porte est encore fermée. Elle demande _____ sa mère : « N'allons-nous pas manger de croissants ce matin? » « Nous sommes arrivées de bonne heure₄! Les croissants ne sont pas encore prêts₅ », répond sa mère. Elles montent _____ café boire un bon chocolat chaud en attendant₆ leurs croissants.

1. Où est-ce qu'Alice va avec sa famille? _____

2. Elle rêve de quoi? _____

3. Que boivent-elles en attendant leurs croissants? _____

1. tout de suite : immediately	*2. se réveiller : to wake up*	*3. s'endormir : to fall asleep*
4. de bonne heure : early	*5. prêt(e) : ready*	*6. en attendant : while waiting*

L'art et la culture

Art and Culture

Vocabulaire : L'art et la culture

Grammaire : Les verbes réfléchis

> **Est-ce que je fais un bon musicien?**
> *Do I make a good musician?*

A. Copiez les mots.
Copy the words.

le cinéma
cinema

_____

luh see·neh·mah

 a filmmaker
un cinéaste

_____

euhn see·neh·ahst

une cinéaste

_____

ewn see·neh·ahst

la poésie
poetry

_____

lah poh·eh·zee

 a poet
un poète

_____

euhn poh·eht

une poète

_____

ewn poh·eht

la peinture
painting

_____

lah pahn·tewr

 a painter
un peintre

_____

euhn pahntr

une peintre

_____

ewn pahntr

la musique
music

_____

lah mew·zeek

 a musician
un musicien

_____

euhn mew·zee·syahn

une musicienne

_____

ewn mew·zee·syehn

le théâtre
theatre

_____

luh teh·ahtr

 an actor/actress
un acteur

_____

euhn ahk·tuhr

une actrice

_____

ewn ahk·treess

la littérature
literature

_____

lah lee·teh·rah·tewr

👧👦 a writer

un écrivain

_____

euhn eh·kree·vahn

une écrivaine

_____

ewn eh·kree·vehn

la cuisine
cooking

_____

lah kwee·zeen

👧👦 a cook

un cuisinier

_____

euhn kwee·zee·nyeh

une cuisinière

_____

ewn kwee·zee·nyehr

la sculpture
sculpture

_____

lah skewl·tewr

👧👦 a sculptor

un sculpteur

_____

euhn skewl·tuhr

une sculpteure

_____

ewn skewl·tuhr

sentir to sense/to feel

_____

saan·teer

je sens	nous sentons
tu sens	vous sentez
il/elle sent	ils/elles sentent

créer to create

_____

kreh·eh

peindre to paint

_____

pahndr

je peins	nous peignons
tu peins	vous peignez
il/elle peint	ils/elles peignent

jouer
to play

_____

joo·eh

composer
to compose

_____

kohm·poh·zeh

réaliser
to produce

_____

reh·ah·lee·zeh

sculpter
to sculpt

_____

skewl·teh

B. Qui fait quoi?
Who does what?

1. Un sculpteur _____

2. Une musicienne _____

3. Un réalisateur _____

4. Un poète _____

5. Une écrivaine _____

6. Un acteur _____

A fait du théâtre.

B écrit de la littérature.

C réalise des films.

D fait des sculptures.

E compose de la poésie.

F joue de la musique.

Les verbes pronominaux
Pronominal Verbs

In French, some verbs are accompanied by a reflexive pronoun (se/s'). These are called pronominal verbs. With pronominal verbs, the action is carried out on the subject.

se laver to wash oneself

singulier		
Je me lave.	I wash myself.
Tu te laves.	You wash yourself.
Il se lave.	He washes himself.
Elle se lave.	She washes herself.

pluriel		
Nous nous lavons.	We wash ourselves.
Vous vous lavez.	You wash yourselves.
Ils se lavent.	They wash themselves.
Elles se lavent.	They wash themselves.

other pronominal verbs

se sentir
to feel (to feel oneself)

se coucher
to go to bed (to put oneself to bed)

se réveiller
to wake up (to wake oneself up)

s'habiller
to dress
(to dress oneself)

s'appeler*
to be called
(to call oneself)

*s'appeler

je m'appelle

tu t'appelles

il/elle s'appelle

nous nous appelons

vous vous appelez

ils/elles s'appellent

C. **Écrivez le bon pronom réfléchi selon le sujet.**
Write the reflexive pronoun that agrees with the subject.

1. Je _____ lave bien quand je prends ma douche.

2. Marie _____ réveille à 9 h pour aller à l'école.

3. Tu _____ appelles Marianne et ta sœur, elle _____ appelle Julie.

4. Il _____ habille chaudement en hiver.

5. Nous _____ couchons à 21 h chaque nuit.

6. Je _____ sens malade quand je mange trop de bonbons.

7. Nous _____ sentons en bonne forme.

L'impératif des verbes réfléchis
Imperative of Reflexives

In the imperative, the subject and the pronominal pronouns become "tonique" pronouns. This means their position changes from before the conjugated verb to after it, and they are introduced by a hyphen.

subject +	pronominal pronouns	tonique
tu	te	toi
nous	nous	nous
vous	vous	vous

e.g. Tu te couches.*
Couche-toi!
Go to bed!

Nous nous habillons.
Habillons-nous!
Let's get dressed/dress ourselves!

Vous vous lavez.
Lavez-vous!
Wash yourselves!

*In the imperative, the "-s" ending is dropped for "-ER" verbs in the 2nd person singular.

Remember, imperative is only expressed in the 2nd person singular and plural (tu, vous) and in the 1st person plural (nous).

D. Transformez les phrases du présent à l'impératif.
Change the present tense sentences into the imperative.

1. Nous nous réveillons tôt le matin. _____

2. Vous vous sentez contents. _____

3. Tu t'habilles bien. _____

4. Tu te couches de bonne heure. _____

5. Nous nous promenons dans la forêt. _____

6. Vous vous couchez. _____

7.

   Tu te laves.

   _____

E. **D'abord, traduisez la phrase littéralement. Ensuite écrivez la même phrase en anglais courant.**
First translate the sentence literally. Then write the same sentence in everyday English.

1. Vous <u>vous amusez</u> toujours au parc.

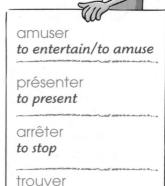

2. Le chameau <u>se trouve</u> dans le désert.

amuser	to entertain/to amuse
présenter	to present
arrêter	to stop
trouver	to find

3. Je <u>m'arrête</u> devant la station du métro.

4. Nous <u>nous présentons</u> à la professeure le premier jour d'école.

F. **Écrivez les phrases au négatif.**
Write the sentences in the negative.

1. Vous vous appelez Mme Leblanc.

2. Je me réveille à 4 h.

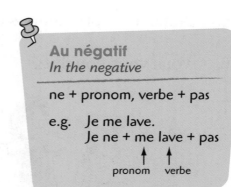

Au négatif
In the negative

ne + pronom, verbe + pas

e.g. Je me lave.
Je ne + me lave + pas
↑   ↑
pronom   verbe

G. Remplissez les tirets en conjuguant les verbes.
Fill in the blanks by conjugating the verbs.

Paul, le cuisinier, _____ tard la nuit et il
                        se coucher

_____ le matin. Il est toujours à l'heure₁
ne se réveiller pas

mais aujourd'hui il _____ au restaurant
                    se rendre : to go to

en retard₂. Puisque₃ c'est dimanche, le restaurant est

plein de monde₄ qui mange le brunch. Les clients de son restaurant ne sont pas

toujours amicaux₅. Les hommes _____ toujours très bien et les
                               s'habiller

femmes _____ belles. Il _____ des gens biens gentils
        se sentir   s'agir

qui sont quelques fois impatients. Ce matin le chef de Paul, un peu stressé lui

dit : « _____ - toi! » Paul _____ ; calmement il répond :
        se dépêcher : to hurry up   ne se fâcher pas

« La cuisine, c'est un art Monsieur! C'est comme la peinture. Il faut être patient

pour avoir un chef-d'œuvre₆! » Ce jour-là, les clients _____
                                                         se trouver : to find oneself

devant les meilleures omelettes au monde!

1. *à l'heure : on time*   2. *en retard : late*   3. *puisque : since*
4. *plein(e) de monde : full of people*   5. *amical(e) : friendly*   6. *un chef-d'œuvre : a masterpiece*

La révision 2

La révision
- Les magasins et leurs produits
- Les verbes du 3ᵉ groupe
- Le journal et les nouvelles
- Les nombres : de l à 1000
- Au musée
- Les médias
- Le transport
- L'art et la culture

A. Écrivez les mots à la bonne place et conjuguez les verbes si nécessaire.
Write the words in the correct space and conjugate the verbs if necessary.

soixante-cinq	Météo	lire	assez	partir	sortir
lait peu jus	le dépanneur		journal	Dessins	aller

A Je vais _____ chez _____ pour chercher du _____ et

du __*jus*__ d'orange pour mon déjeuner.

B Chaque samedi, je __*lire*__ mon livre de mon sac et je _____

pendant deux heures. Ensuite je _____ pour ma leçon de danse.

C Le matin, ma famille partage les sections du _____ . Moi, je prends la

section « __*Dessins*__ » car j'aime les bandes dessinées. Mon père cherche

toujours le temps dans la section « __*Météo*__ ».

D Elle n'a jamais _____ d'argent pour payer ses factures. Elle travaille

__*soixante-cinq*__ heures par semaine. Elle a _____ de congé.

time off

le gros titre	billets	artiste	peintures	musée
billetterie	plan	pied	autobus	journal

E **F** **G** **H**

E Vous pouvez acheter vos _____ et un _____ du _____ à la _____ .

F On trouve _____ sur la première page du _____ .

G Je vais à l'école en _____ . C'est beaucoup plus rapide que d'y aller à _____ .

H L' _____ crée des _____ .

B. Écrivez vrai ou faux.
Write true or false.

1. La cuisinière se trouve dans le salon. _____

2. On achète un pantalon chez la boucherie. _____

3. Vous lisez ce qui est écrit. _____

4. On peut chercher un nouvel emploi dans la section « Cinéma ». _____

5. On sort par la sortie. _____

6. On vend des tartes au citron à la boutique. _____

C. Écrivez le bon mot français dans le tiret.
Write the correct French word in the blank.

C'est la fin de semaine et moi et ma sœur

lisons 1._____ parce que nous voulons

2._____ ce qu'il y a à faire. Nous

3._____ sortir 4._____ mais

nous ne savons pas où aller. 5._____ sœur 6._____ vouloir

aller au marché. « Je viens de lire dans la section 7._____ qu'il y a

8._____ de l'alimentation fantastique au marché! » dit-elle. Ma sœur

sait que j'aime 9._____ manger. « Allons-y! » Une fois au marché,

nous 10._____ un groupe de personnes autour d'une grande table.

Nous ne 11._____ pas voir ce qu'elles regardent. « Nous sommes

12._____ loin; nous 13._____ nous rapprocher! » De plus

près, nous 14._____ une longue 15._____ . Tout d'un coup, le

boulanger crie : « J'ai réussi! C'est la baguette la plus longue au monde! Elle mesure

plus de 16._____ mètres. Elle va être exposée au 17._____ la

semaine prochaine! » Avec mes yeux fixés sur le pain délicieux je demande :

« 18._____ cette baguette précieuse? » « Êtes-vous malade? » demande-

t-il. « Elle n'est pas en vente! Ne 19._____ pas mon chef-d'œuvre! »

dit-il d'un air très fier. « Nous venons de 20._____ une après-midi trop

amusante », dit ma sœur en riant.

1.	the newspaper	2.	to know	3.	to want (to)	4.	by bike
5.	my	6.	to admit (to)	7.	culture	8.	an exhibition
9.	well	10.	to notice	11.	to be able (to)	12.	too (much)
13.	to have (to)	14.	to observe	15.	baguette	16.	seventy-five
17.	museum	18.	how much does __ cost	19.	to touch	20.	to spend (time)

D. Remettez le texte en ordre.
Put the events from the text in order.

1. Ils se rapprochent de la grande table.
2. Ils lisent le journal.
3. Le boulanger annonce sa réussite.
4. Il essaie de toucher la baguette.
5. Ils partent pour le marché.
6. Ils remarquent des gens autour d'une table.

_____

_____

_____

_____

_____

E. Encerclez la bonne réponse.
Circle the correct answer.

1. Une boutique vend...
     A
    B
    C

2. Il veut dormir.
     A
    B
    C

3. Le prix du billet est cent quarante dollars.
     A

Musée du Louvre
104 $

     B

Musée du Louvre
140 $

     C

Musée du Louvre
40 $

4. C'est une émission radiophonique.
     A
     B
    C

F. **Écrivez la bonne lettre dans le cercle.**
Write the correct letter in the circle.

On dort... ◯

Nous voyageons... ◯

L'Internet est... ◯

La caissière travaille... ◯

La voiture coûte... ◯

Ils se lavent... ◯

Les nouvelles se trouvent... ◯

On écrit... ◯

On conduit... ◯

Les musées exposent... ◯

Les gâteaux sont... ◯

Les spectateurs regardent... ◯

A dans la baignoire.

B à l'épicerie.

C très chère.

D avec un stylo.

E dans un lit.

F une voiture.

G en bateau.

H dans le journal.

I l'écran.

J un réseau public.

K bon marché.

L des collections historiques.

G. Rayez l'intrus.
Cross out the word that does not belong.

le pain	dormir	cinq cents	la radio
le biscuit	lire	deux cents	l'auditeur
l'écrivain	partir	six cents	le journal
la baguette	sortir	trente-deux	l'auditrice
en avion	le poète	la chronique	les pantoufles
en métro	le film	l'atelier	les sandales
en bateau	le réalisateur	le gros titre	les gants
à cheval	le cinéma	le sous-titre	les chaussures

H. Associez les nombres en lettres aux chiffres.
Link the number words with the digits.

1. cinq cent soixante et onze • • 237
2. trois cent dix • • 452
3. mille deux • • 916
4. deux cent trente-sept • • 122
5. neuf cent seize • • 764
6. six cent quatre-vingt-neuf • • 310
7. quatre cent cinquante-deux • • 571
8. sept cent soixante-quatre • • 848
9. cent vingt-deux • • 1002
10. huit cent quarante-huit • • 689

L'heure du conte

Le cœur du singe

Personnages

le singe

le crocodile

**la femme
crocodile**

Près d'une large **rivière** dans une jungle sauvage vit un singe très **sage**.

Regarde! Il y a un singe sur la branche.

Dans la même rivière vivent deux des plus grands et plus méchants crocodiles. Ils se croient le roi et la reine de la rivière et quand ils voient le singe ils veulent le manger pour le **dîner**.

Réponses courtes

1. Est-ce que le singe vit dans une forêt ou dans une jungle?

2. Qu'est-ce que les crocodiles veulent manger pour le dîner?

Un jour, les crocodiles décident que c'est le jour spécial pour manger le singe. Le singe est toujours sur la branche et il mange un fruit calmement. Il voit les crocodiles mais il pense qu'ils sont des **gentils** crocodiles.

Chéri, je veux manger le cœur du singe pour le dîner.

Ma mère est gentille. Elle me prépare le dîner.
My mom is kind. She prepares dinner for me.

Nouveaux mots
New Words

la rivière : river   *sage : wise*

le dîner : dinner

gentil(le) : kind, nice

Le crocodile crée un plan pour duper le singe et manger son cœur. Le crocodile et sa femme sont des créatures très patientes.

Il **attend** voir le singe descendre de l'arbre. Le singe a soif et il boit beaucoup d'eau sans voir le crocodile.

Réponses courtes

1. Qu'est-ce que le crocodile fait?

2. Pourquoi est-ce que le singe ne peut pas traverser la rivière?

« Singe, pourquoi est-ce que tu habites de cette côté de la rivière? » le crocodile **demande** au singe. « Le fruit de l'autre côté de la rivière est plus doux et plus grand qu'ici. » Le crocodile **essaie** de **convaincre** le singe d'aller de l'autre côté de la rivière.

Je sais, mais la rivière est trop large et je ne peux pas nager.

Je convaincs mon père de m'acheter un téléphone portable.
I convince my dad to buy me a cell phone.

Nouveaux verbes
New Verbs

attendre : *to wait*

demander : *to ask*   *essayer* : *to try*

convaincre : *to convince*

Le singe est ravi et il accepte l'offre du crocodile.
Sans hésiter, il monte **sur le dos** du crocodile pour traverser
la rivière. Le crocodile nage lentement et doucement sans
faire peur au singe. Le singe est très content et s'imagine
manger les fruits de l'autre côté de la rivière.

Réponses courtes

1. Comment est-ce que le singe traverse la rivière?

2. Pourquoi est-ce que le crocodile plonge sous l'eau?

Soudainement, le crocodile plonge sous l'eau et le singe se bat pour ne pas noyer. Il ne peut pas respirer et il a très peur.

Pourquoi fais-tu ça?

Le crocodile dit avec un sourire méchant : « Tu ne dois pas faire confiance aux crocodiles. Je vais te noyer et manger ton cœur pour le dîner. »

Tu me fais peur tout le temps.
You scare me all the time.

Nouvelles expressions
New Expressions

sans hésiter : without hesitating
sur le dos : on the back
faire peur : to scare, to frighten

Le singe sait qu'il est en grave danger et essaie de penser vite. « Qu'est-ce que je vais faire? » il se demande.

Une idée lui **vient à l'esprit** pour se sauver. Il lui dit : « Les singes ne gardent pas leur cœur dans le corps, ils le gardent dans les arbres. » Le crocodile réfléchit **pendant un long moment**.

Réponses courtes

1. Qu'est-ce que le singe fait pour se sauver?

2. Qu'est-ce que le singe accepte de faire?

Le crocodile croit ce que le singe lui dit et pense à un nouveau plan deux fois plus méchant que le premier.

Montre-moi où se trouve ton cœur et je vais t'**épargner la vie**.

Le singe accepte de lui montrer où se trouve son cœur et le crocodile le porte sur son dos pour l'amener à l'autre côté. Le singe est soulagé une fois sur le dos du crocodile car il peut respirer.

Partez maintenant. J'épargne votre vie.
Leave now. I spare your life.

Nouvelles expressions
New Expressions

venir à l'esprit : to come to mind

pendant un long moment : for a long time

épargner la vie : to spare a life

Une fois qu'ils **s'approchent** du bord de la rivière, le singe saute immédiatement du dos du crocodile. Il **grimpe** rapidement le figuier, l'arbre avec des figues et non pas de cœurs. Le crocodile est si fâché mais **se rend compte** qu'il est dupé. Il essaie de convaincre le singe de descendre de l'arbre mais ne peut pas.

Je t'ai dupé!

Descends de là!

Réponses courtes

1. Comment se sent le crocodile quand il est dupé?

2. Comment est-ce que le singe décrit le crocodile?

Le singe jette des figues qui frappent le pauvre crocodile sur la tête et lui dit : « Tu es peut-être grand et tout-puissant mais tu n'es pas trop intelligent. »

Le crocodile ne peut pas le croire. Son « dîner » se moque de lui, l'insulte et jette des figues. Il ne sait pas quoi faire et il n'est plus fâché, il est triste.

Je m'approche de la souris sans bruit.
I approach the mouse silently.

Nouveaux verbes
New Verbs

s'approcher : to approach
grimper : to climb
se rendre compte : to realize

> Comment est-ce que c'est possible de vivre sans un cœur dans le corps? C'est bête!

Réponses courtes

1. Est-ce que le singe s'arrête de se moquer du crocodile?

2. Comment se sent le crocodile à la fin?

Le singe ne s'arrête pas de se moquer du crocodile. Il veut s'assurer que le crocodile comprend son erreur.

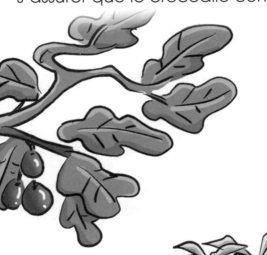

Le crocodile se sent **triste** parce que non seulement il perd son dîner mais il se sent bête aussi. Il se dit : « Je ne vais jamais essayer de duper ce singe encore. » Il regrette encore plus ses actions et dit qu'il va changer.

Ce n'est pas une **grande** surprise!

Coin de grammaire
Grammar Corner

Un adjectif décrit un nom et en général change en genre (masculin ou féminin) et en nombre (quantité). Il y a des exceptions à la règle qui changent en nombre mais pas en genre. On écrit et on prononce ces adjectifs de la même manière.

S	P	S	P
grand	grand**s**	grand**e**	grand**es**
*triste	triste**s**	*triste	triste**s**

Observe que la forme féminine et masculine ne changent pas.

Est-ce que tu te rappelles?

Remplis les espaces pour compléter les phrases. Ensuite mets les événements en ordre.

Fill in the blanks to complete the sentences. Then put the events in order.

A. Le crocodile se sent _____ parce que non seulement il perd son dîner mais il se sent bête aussi.

cœur

se moquer

triste

sur le dos

respirer

crée

B. Le singe sait qu'il est en grave danger et convainc le crocodile que son _____ est dans l'arbre.

C. Le singe accepte l'offre du crocodile et sans hésiter monte _____ du crocodile.

D. Le crocodile _____ un plan pour duper le singe et le convaincre d'aller de l'autre côté de la rivière.

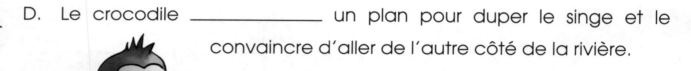

E. Soudainement, le crocodile plonge sous l'eau et le singe ne peut pas _____ .

F. Dans l'arbre, le singe ne s'arrête pas de _____ du crocodile.

Ordre d'événements

Corrige les erreurs

Corrige les erreurs d'orthographe et de conjugaison dans le paragraphe suivant.
Correct the spelling and conjugation errors in the following paragraph.

> **Orthographe : 10**
> **Conjugaison : 10**

Dans la river vit deux crocodile grand et méchant qui croit qu'ils vont manger le couer du sing. Le singe voient les crocodiles et pensent qu'ils est gentil. Le crocodile créons un plan pour dupe le singe et le mange. Mais le singe est plus sages que les crocodiles et apprend sa leçon qu'il ne peux pas faire confiance au crocodiles. À la fin, quand il voyons sa femme, il se sent trist.

Conjuguons ensemble

Complète les conjugaisons. Ensuite remplis les espaces avec la bonne conjugaison en utilisant « créer » ou « croire ».

Complete the conjugations. Then fill in the blanks with the correct conjugation using "to create" or "to believe".

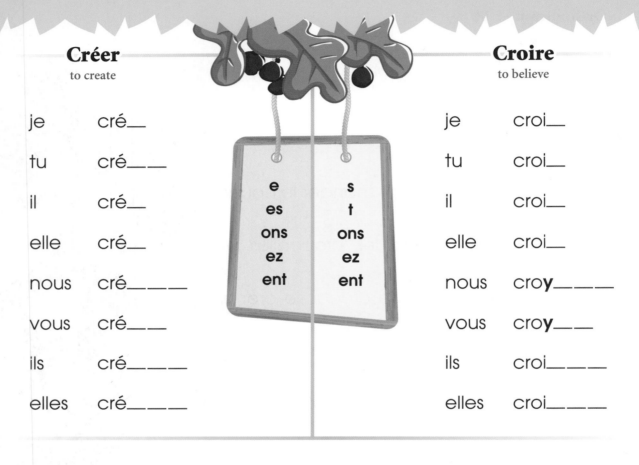

Créer
to create

je	cré__
tu	cré___
il	cré__
elle	cré__
nous	cré_____
vous	cré___
ils	cré_____
elles	cré_____

e
es
ons
ez
ent

s
t
ons
ez
ent

Croire
to believe

je	croi__
tu	croi__
il	croi__
elle	croi__
nous	croy_____
vous	croy___
ils	croi_____
elles	croi_____

1. _____
   I believe

2. _____
   Sam and Anne create

3. _____
   Mrs. Smith creates

4. _____
   Molly believes

5. _____
   you and Adam create

6. _____
   Jack and Joy believe

7. _____
   Lisa and I create

8. Tu _____ ce que je te dis.

Conjuguons ensemble

Remplis les espaces à l'aide du tableau sur la page de gauche.
Fill in the blanks with the help of the table on the left page.

1. Les crocodiles _____ qu'ils vont manger le cœur du singe pour le dîner.

2. Est-ce que le plan que le crocodile _____ pour duper le singe fonctionne à la fin?

3. Le singe dit aux crocodiles : « Le plan que vous _____ ne va pas fonctionner! »

4. Le crocodile _____ qu'il est le roi de la rivière et sa femme la reine.

5. Le crocodile _____ ce que le singe lui dit.

6. Nous _____ une fin alternative à l'histoire!

7. Je _____ que vous pouvez le faire.

Résumé de l'histoire

Fais un résumé de l'histoire « Le cœur du singe » à l'aide de la phrase et des mots donnés.

Summarize the story "The Monkey's Heart" with the help of the given sentence and words.

convaincre

se moquer

sans hésiter

les figues

grimper

triste

Le crocodile et sa femme créent un plan pour manger le cœur du singe.

Un jour, _____

_____

_____

_____

_____

_____

_____

Histoire **2**

L'aventure du petit ânon

Personnages

l'homme

son fils

le petit ânon

Sur une petite ferme vit un homme avec son fils. Un jour son ânesse **donne naissance à** un petit ânon. Ils doivent décider ce qu'ils vont faire avec lui. Leur ferme est très petite et ils n'ont pas **assez de** nourriture pour les deux animaux.

Réponses courtes

1. Comment est-ce qu'on appelle la femelle de l'âne?

2. Où est-ce que l'homme et son fils vont vendre le petit ânon?

Finalement, l'homme a une idée. Il décide que puisqu'il n'a pas besoin de deux ânes, il doit vendre le petit ânon au marché. L'homme et son fils commencent à se préparer pour le marché. Ils doivent décider **quel** chemin prendre pour y arriver et aussi à quel prix vendre le petit ânon.

Mon fils, je pense que nous devons vendre le petit ânon.

Je pense que tu as raison, Papa.

Je pense que cette bague est assez grande pour moi.
I think that this ring is big enough for me.

Nouvelles expressions
New Expressions

donner naissance à : to give birth to

assez (de) : enough (of)

quel(le) : which

Le marché est très loin et l'homme et son fils savent qu'il ne va pas être facile d'y arriver. Ils préparent quelques **provisions** et sont prêts à se mettre en **chemin**. L'homme ne veut pas fatiguer le petit ânon donc lui et son fils décident de le porter attaché par ses **sabots** à un long bâton. L'ânon n'est pas facile à porter parce qu'il est très **lourd** et le chemin est difficile.

Pourquoi me portent-ils comme ça? Je préfère marcher.

Réponses courtes

1. Comment est-ce que l'homme et son fils décident de porter l'ânon?

2. Pourquoi est-ce que les villageois se moquent de l'homme et son fils?

Quand ils arrivent à un village, tous les villageois regardent l'homme et son fils et ne peuvent pas en croire leurs yeux. L'homme et son fils portent l'ânon quand c'est l'ânon qui doit porter l'homme et son fils. Les villageois se moquent d'eux.

C'est l'âne qui doit porter l'homme et non pas l'homme qui doit porter l'âne!

Oh non! Le chemin est bloqué!
Oh no! The path is blocked!

Nouveaux mots
New Words

la provision : supply

le chemin : path

le sabot : hoof   *lourd : heavy*

Ils ont raison mon fils.

Une fois loin des villageois, l'homme dit à son fils qu'ils ont raison. Alors il dit à son fils de **détacher** l'ânon et de se mettre sur son dos. Maintenant ils vont marcher plus facilement et ils vont arriver au marché plus rapidement. Le fils est très content parce qu'il ne doit plus porter l'ânon.

Réponses courtes

1. Est-ce que l'homme est d'accord avec les villageois?

2. Pourquoi est-ce que la femme gronde le fils?

Quand ils arrivent au prochain village, ils **rencontrent** une vieille femme et son chien.

« Tu es un garçon si égoïste », elle **gronde** le fils. « Ton père est plus âgé que toi et tu dois lui montrer du respect! C'est lui qui doit monter sur l'ânon et non pas toi », elle lui dit.

Je pense qu'elle a raison mon fils. Descends et je vais monter.

Détache-moi! Je te donnerai tout mon fromage.
Untie me! I will give you all my cheese.

Nouveaux verbes
New Verbs

détacher : *to untie*
rencontrer : *to meet*
gronder : *to scold*

Le fils pense que la femme **a raison** quand elle dit que son père doit monter sur l'ânon. Il saute de l'ânon et il aide son père à monter sur l'ânon. Les deux continuent sur leur chemin au marché avec l'homme sur le dos de l'ânon et son fils **à ses côtés**.

N'oublie pas ce que je dis.

Réponses courtes

1. Est-ce que le fils fait ce que la vieille femme lui dit?

2. Où est-ce qu'ils rencontrent la jeune fille?

Peu après, ils rencontrent une jeune fille qui vient chercher de l'eau du puits. Elle regarde l'homme et son fils avec confusion. Elle ne comprend pas pourquoi l'ânon porte l'homme et **non pas** son fils. Elle devient de plus en plus fâchée. « Votre fils est trop jeune, c'est lui que l'ânon doit porter et non pas vous », dit la jeune fille.

Oh non! Pas encore.

Tu as raison. Je dois étudier plus.
You are right. I have to study more.

Nouvelles expressions
New Expressions

avoir raison : to be right　　*à son côté : by his side*
peu après : soon after　　*non pas : not*

L'homme ne descend pas de l'ânon parce qu'il a une idée.
« Monte avec moi, l'ânon est assez fort pour nous porter tous les
deux », il dit à son fils. Le fils n'est pas sûr que le pauvre ânon peut
les porter tous les deux mais il écoute toujours son père et monte sur
le dos de l'ânon.

Réponses courtes

1. Qui suggère l'idée de monter l'ânon?

2. Pourquoi est-ce que le fermier crie à l'homme et à son fils?

Quand ils arrivent à un **champ de maïs**, ils entendent les **cris** d'un fermier. Au début ils sont trop loin pour l'entendre **clairement**, mais quand ils s'approchent le fermier continue à crier et son message est plus clair.

Hé! Ce pauvre ânon est trop petit et trop jeune pour vous porter tous les deux!

Je vis dans un champ de maïs.
I live in a cornfield.

Nouveaux mots
New Words

un champ de maïs : cornfield
un cri : shout
clairement : clearly

Finalement, l'homme et son fils décident de descendre et mener l'ânon pour le reste du chemin au marché.

Quand ils arrivent au marché, une famille **très** gentille achète l'ânon. L'homme et son fils peuvent finalement respirer tranquillement. Ils sont contents et soulagés.

J'espère que votre famille va aimer l'ânon.

Réponses courtes

1. Qui achète finalement l'ânon?

2. Qu'est-ce qui indique que l'homme et son fils sont soulagés à la fin?

Sur le chemin de retour à la maison, l'homme et son fils discutent leur longue journée. Ils écoutent pour voir s'il y a des cris des personnes sur la route mais n'entendent rien cette fois. Le fils écoute tout ce que son père dit avec attention et pense qu'il a raison.

C'est **vraiment** très bête d'écouter à tout le monde.

C'est vrai, Papa. C'est impossible de plaire à tout le monde.

Il écoute **toujours** son père.

Le fils est **très** content.

C'est **vraiment** très bête.

Finalement, l'homme et son fils sont très confus.

Coin de grammaire
Grammar Corner

*Un adverbe** modifie le plus souvent :

- *un verbe*
- *un adjectif*
- *un adverbe*
- *toute la phrase*

*Parfois on peut reconnaître l'adverbe par sa terminaison en -**ment**. Ex : Finale**ment**.

Est-ce que tu te rappelles?

Remplis les espaces pour compléter les phrases. Ensuite mets les événements en ordre.

Fill in the blanks to complete the sentences. Then put the events in order.

A.   Un homme et son fils décident de vendre l'ânon au _____ .

villageois	monter	l'ânon
vendent	marché	fermier

B.   Quand ils rencontrent une jeune fille, elle leur dit que c'est le fils que _____ doit porter.

C.   Au prochain village, une vieille femme dit que c'est l'homme qui doit _____ sur l'ânon.

D.   Au marché, ils _____ l'ânon et de retour à la maison ils pensent que c'est impossible de plaire à tout le monde.

E.   Quand ils arrivent à un champ de maïs, un _____ leur crie que l'ânon est trop petit pour les porter.

F.   Au premier village, les _____ pensent que c'est l'ânon qui doit porter l'homme et son fils.

Ordre d'événements

☐ ☐ ☐ ☐ ☐ ☐

Qui a dit quoi?

Quels personnages de l'histoire ont dit les phrases suivantes? Relie la phrase au personnage qui correspond.

Which characters from the story said the following sentences? Match the sentence with the corresponding character.

A. « Tu es un garçon si égoïste…Ton père est plus âgé que toi et tu dois lui montrer du respect! »

B. « Hé! Ce pauvre ânon est trop petit et trop jeune pour vous porter tous les deux! »

C. « C'est l'âne qui doit porter l'homme et non pas l'homme qui doit porter l'âne. »

D. « Votre fils est trop jeune, c'est lui que l'ânon doit porter et non pas vous. »

E. « Pourquoi me portent-ils comme ça? Je préfère marcher. »

F. « Mon fils, je pense que nous devons vendre le petit ânon. »

Conjuguons ensemble

Complète les conjugaisons. Ensuite remplis les espaces avec la bonne conjugaison en utilisant « écouter » ou « entendre ».

Complete the conjugations. Then fill in the blanks with the correct conjugation using "to listen" or "to hear".

Écouter		Entendre	
to listen		to hear	
j'	écout__	j'	entend__
tu	écout___	tu	entend__
il	écout__	il	entend
elle	écout__	elle	entend
nous	écout____	nous	entend_____
vous	écout___	vous	entend___
ils	écout_____	ils	entend_____
elles	écout____	elles	entend_____

Center bubble (left): e / es / ons / ez / ent

Center bubble (right): s / ons / ez / ent

1. _____
   May and Molly hear

2. _____
   she listens

3. _____
   you and Alex listen

4. _____
   Carrie and I hear

5. _____
   my mom hears

6. _____
   Seth and Gemma listen

7. _____
   I listen

8. _____
   Uncle Phil hears

9

Le fils _____ tout ce que son père dit avec attention.

Conjuguons ensemble

Remplis les espaces à l'aide du tableau sur la page de gauche.
Fill in the blanks with the help of the table on the left page.

1. L'homme et son fils _____ toutes les personnes sur leur chemin.

2. Ils _____ les cris d'un fermier mais il est trop loin et ce n'est pas clair.

3. Le fils _____ et fait tout ce que son père lui dit car il est sage.

4. « Est-ce que vous _____ ? Descendez de l'ânon! » crie la femme.

5. « Papa, j'_____ ce que tu dis parce que je suis un bon fils », dit le garçon.

6. Si tu lis l'histoire avec attention, est-ce que tu _____ le message?

L'aventure du petit ânon

Toi

7. Oui, j'_____ . Le message de l'histoire est _____ _____ .

Résumé de l'histoire

Fais un résumé de l'histoire « L'aventure du petit ânon » à l'aide de la phrase et des mots donnés.

Summarize the story "The Donkey's Journey" with the help of the given sentence and words.

avoir raison

le marché

descendre

la journée

le chemin

monter

Pourquoi portez-vous l'ânon?

Dans le premier village, les villageois

se moquent l'homme et son fils parce

qu'ils portent l'ânon. Peu après, _____

_____

_____

_____

_____

_____

_____

Histoire 3

Une découverte près de la mer

Personnages

Charles

Christophe et Jeanne

les pirates

Un beau jour **ensoleillé**, Christophe, Jeanne et Charles vont à la plage. Ils veulent tout faire pour s'amuser et ils commencent avec une **promenade** près de la mer.

3

Cette coquille va parfaitement ici!

Réponses courtes

1. Qu'est-ce que Jeanne utilise pour décorer le château?

2. Pourquoi est-ce que Jeanne commence à pleurer?

Ils commencent à construire un **château de sable**. Jeanne utilise les coquilles trouvées sur la plage pour décorer le château.

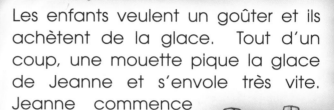

Les enfants veulent un goûter et ils achètent de la glace. Tout d'un coup, une mouette pique la glace de Jeanne et s'envole très vite. Jeanne commence à pleurer.

Comme c'est beau!

Ça va, Jeanne. Je vais t'en chercher une autre.

Je fais une promenade sur la plage avec mon ours en peluche.
I go for a walk on the beach with my teddy bear.

Nouveaux mots
New Words

ensoleillé(e) : sunny

une promenade : walk

un château de sable : sandcastle

Les enfants commencent à attraper des **tous petits** crabes. Charles essaye d'attraper un petit crabe vert mais le crabe le pince et lui **fait mal** au doigt. Il pleure un peu mais s'arrête parce qu'il est un grand garçon. Christophe trouve ce qui se passe très amusant et se rit de Charles.

Ce petit crabe paraît **vraiment** fâché!

Réponses courtes

1. Qu'est-ce que le petit crabe vert fait à Charles?

2. Qu'est-ce que Jeanne compte?

Christophe saute dans l'eau et Charles après lui. Jeanne ne nage pas. Elle est en train d'attraper des crevettes avec son filet.

Un, deux, trois…

La lumière du soleil fait mal aux yeux.
The sunlight hurts the eyes.

Nouvelles expressions
New Expressions

tout petit : very small

faire mal : to hurt

vraiment : really, very

Soudainement, des gros nuages de pluie **couvrent** le soleil et la mer et le ciel deviennent gris. La pluie commence à tomber et les enfants **courent** pour s'abriter mais ils ne voient aucun abri. Charles est le premier à voir une grotte et il dit aux autres. Les amis courent et entrent dans la grotte. Ils sont si contents d'être à l'abri.

Courez vite, il y a une grotte un peu plus loin!

Réponses courtes

1. Pourquoi est-ce que les enfants courent à la grotte?

2. Qu'est-ce que les enfants trouvent dans un coin de la grotte?

Charles veut explorer et il convainc Christophe et Jeanne d'aller avec lui. Dans un coin de la grotte ils voient quelque chose qui **brille**…ils **trouvent** un coffre rempli de trésors! Dans le coffre il y a des pièces d'or, des bagues, des colliers et d'autres objets précieux. Les amis ont peur de toucher les trésors et se demandent pourquoi ce coffre se trouve ici.

Ouah! Regarde ce que nous avons trouvé!

Tes yeux brillent comme des diamants!
Your eyes shine like diamonds!

Nouveaux verbes
New Verbs

couvrir : *to cover*   courir : *to run*

briller : *to shine*   trouver : *to find*

Puis, ils entendent des voix et ils sont choqués quand ils voient qu'ils sont **entourés** par des pirates...des pirates aux **barbes** longues, avec des **épées** et des **couteaux**. Ils sont en train de rire fortement et regarder les enfants avec des yeux méchants. Les enfants ont très peur et ne savent pas où aller ou comment s'échapper.

Réponses courtes

1. Qu'est-ce que les enfants entendent?

2. Pourquoi est-ce que les enfants ont peur?

Tout d'un coup, des lumières brillantes éclairent la grotte entière. Saisis de peur, les enfants ne bougent pas. Encore une fois, ils ne savent pas quoi faire. Les trois ont trop peur d'ouvrir les yeux. Ils peuvent entendre des voix et des rires étranges.

Charles, qu'est-ce qui se passe? J'ai vraiment peur!

Regarde-moi, Sally. Ma barbe est si longue!
Look at me, Sally. My beard is so long!

Nouveaux mots
New Words

entouré(e) : surrounded

une barbe : beard

une épée : sword   *un couteau : knife*

Un des pirates rit et dit aux enfants d'ouvrir les yeux. Il explique qu'ils sont en train de **tourner un film** de pirates. « **N'ayez pas peur** les enfants, c'est juste un film et nous ne sommes pas des vrais pirates », il leur dit.

Réponses courtes

1. Qu'est-ce que les pirates font?

2. Qu'est-ce que c'est l'expérience inoubliable pour les amis?

Le réalisateur laisse les enfants rester et regarder le reste du tournage du film. Ils regardent avec intérêt les scènes de bataille et Christophe adore **en particulier** le duel à l'épée entre deux pirates. Quelle expérience inoubliable pour les amis!

N'ayez pas peur. Bruce est très gentil!
Don't be afraid. Bruce is very nice!

Nouvelles expressions
New Expressions

tourner un film : to shoot a movie

n'ayez pas peur : don't be afraid

en particulier : especially

Quand le réalisateur crie « Coupé! », les enfants savent que le tournage est terminé. Ils sont un peu tristes que l'expérience se finit. Un des pirates vient pour donner **à chaque enfant** un petit trésor du coffre. Il donne des pièces de monnaie aux **garçons** et un **très** beau collier à Jeanne. Elle est si contente de ce cadeau qu'elle se le met tout de suite.

Ouah! Comme c'est joli!

Réponses courtes

1. Est-ce que Jeanne aime le cadeau qu'elle reçoit?

2. Qu'est-ce que les enfants voient dans le ciel?

Un peu tristes, les amis partent de la grotte. La pluie arrêtée, le soleil sorti encore, les enfants pensent que c'est une belle **journée**.

Dans le ciel il y a même un arc-en-ciel.

Ouah! Quelle **découverte** incroyable!

Les accents les plus communs sont :

l'accent aigu
se prononce avec la bouche grande ouverte

l'accent grave
ne change pas la prononciation

la cédille
indique que « c » se prononce « s » après a, o, u

Coin de grammaire
Grammar Corner

Exemples :

- journ**é**e
- d**é**couverte

- tr**è**s
- **à** chaque enfant

- o**ù**
- gar**ç**on
- **ç**a

Les accents changent parfois la prononciation d'une lettre et permettent une bonne lecture de la langue.

Est-ce que tu te rappelles?

Remplis les espaces pour compléter les phrases. Ensuite mets les événements en ordre.

Fill in the blanks to complete the sentences. Then put the events in order.

A. Un beau jour _____ , les trois amis vont à la plage et construisent un château de sable.

B. Un des pirates explique qu'ils sont en train de _____ un film.

C. Puis, ils entendent des voix…ce sont des _____ pirates aux barbes longues.

D. Quand des gros nuages couvrent le soleil, ils courent et entrent dans une _____ pour s'abriter.

E. Le réalisateur laisse les enfants regarder le reste du tournage du film. C'est une expérience _____ !

F. Dans un coin, ils trouvent un coffre rempli de _____ !

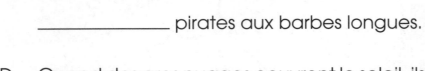

trésors

grotte

inoubliable

ensoleillé

méchants

tourner

Ordre d'événements

☐ ☐ ☐ ☐ ☐ ☐

À l'écrit

Mets les mots dans le bon ordre pour former des phrases complètes.

Put the words in the correct order to form complete sentences.

A   pas   ont   et   savent   comment   très   **Les enfants**   s'échapper   peur   ne

B   la   plage   **Jeanne**   les   château   utilise   coquilles   sur   décorer   le   pour

C   grotte   à   voir   aux   une   **Charles**   est   premier   il   et   dit   autres   le

D   d'un   lumières   grotte   éclairent   **Tout**   coup   des   la   brillantes

E   se   finit   tristes   un   l'expérience   peu   **Ils**   que   sont

A _____

B _____

C _____

D _____

E _____

Conjuguons ensemble

Complète les conjugaisons. Ensuite remplis les espaces avec la bonne conjugaison en utilisant « donner » ou « commencer ».

Complete the conjugations. Then fill in the blanks with the correct conjugation using "to give" or "to begin".

Donner
to give

je   donn__

tu   donn___

il   donn__

elle   donn__

nous   donn____

vous   donn___

ils   donn____

elles   donn____

e
es
ons
ez
ent

Commencer
to begin

je   commenc__

tu   commenc___

il   commenc__

elle   commenc__

nous   commenç____

vous   commenc___

ils   commenc____

elles   commenc____

1. _____
   Blake and I give

2. _____
   you begin

3. _____
   he gives

4. _____
   you and Mary begin

5. _____
   Mr. and Mrs. Green give

6. _____
   Colin and Dean begin

7. Tu me _____ un collier!

Conjuguons ensemble

Remplis les espaces à l'aide du tableau sur la page de gauche.
Fill in the blanks with the help of the table on the left page.

1. Jeanne _____ quelques coquilles aux garçons parce qu'ils n'en trouvent pas.

2. Les trois amis _____ leur journée à la plage avec une promenade.

3. La pluie _____ à tomber et les enfants courent à la grotte pour s'abriter.

4. Comme cadeaux, ils _____ des pièces de monnaie aux garçons et un très beau collier à Jeanne.

5. Jeanne _____ à pleurer parce qu'une mouette pique sa glace et s'envole très vite.

6. Je te _____ un balai. Nettoie le désordre!

7. Je _____ tout de suite, je promets!

Histoire 3

Résumé de l'histoire

Fais un résumé de l'histoire « Une découverte près de la mer » à l'aide de la phrase et des mots donnés.

Summarize the story "A Discovery by the Sea" with the help of the given sentence and words.

trouver

la grotte

tout d'un coup

inoubliable

entendre

le coffre

C'est un beau jour ensoleillé mais soudainement la pluie commence à

tomber et les trois amis courent pour s'abriter. _____

_____

_____

_____

_____

_____

La journée d'Amélie au parc d'attractions

Personnages

Papa et Maman   **Amélie**   **la princesse**

Un samedi matin, Amélie va aller au parc d'attractions pour la première fois avec ses parents. Elle est si enthousiaste et elle veut aller sur tous les **manèges** mais elle sait que ses parents n'ont pas assez d'**argent** pour tous les manèges et peuvent seulement lui en offrir un.

C'est tellement difficile de choisir. Je vais essayer le **Royaume** Enchanté!

Réponses courtes

1. Pourquoi est-ce qu'Amélie ne peut pas aller sur tous les manèges?

2. Qu'est-ce que les enfants font sur la Danse des Sirènes?

Amélie regarde les enfants sur la Danse des Sirènes qui rient, crient avec joie et s'éclaboussent dans l'eau à la fin du manège. Ensuite elle passe par le **Château** de la Princesse. Elle veut entrer là aussi pour rencontrer la princesse.

Ouah! Cela paraît amusant aussi!

Maman, regarde! J'aime bien le Château de la Princesse.

Le château est ruiné de nouveau.
The castle is ruined again.

Nouveaux mots
New Words

le manège : ride

l'argent : money

le royaume : kingdom

le château : castle

Elle continue à explorer les manèges du parc et voit la Grande Ourse qui **a l'air** de descendre très rapidement. **À côté**, elle voit le Grand Carrousel avec des beaux chevaux blancs, bruns et noirs qui tournent et tournent.

Regarde les beaux chevaux!

Réponses courtes

1. Où est-ce qu'on peut trouver les chevaux?

2. Qu'est-ce qu'il y a dans le tunnel?

Finalement, Amélie choisit le manège final, la Maison Hantée. Elle veut essayer ce manège étrange avec ses parents car elle a peur.

Le train entre dans un tunnel sinistre et les plonge dans le noir. Amélie et ses parents entendent des cris et ensuite ils passent par des fantômes, des monstres et des chauves-souris. Quel manège amusant et effrayant **à la fois**!

Nouvelles expressions
New Expressions

Je peux jongler et faire du monocycle à la fois.
I can juggle and ride a unicycle at the same time.

avoir l'air : to seem

à côté : nearby

à la fois : at the same time

Après la Maison Hantée, Amélie et ses parents vont prendre une petite pause. Ils vont ensemble au café pour prendre du thé et des goûters.

Quand c'est le temps de **rentrer** à la maison, Amélie se perd et ne peut pas **retrouver** son chemin. Elle découvre qu'elle est seule dans le parc et non seulement ça...elle est enfermée dans le parc!

Réponses courtes

1.   Où est-ce qu'Amélie et ses parents vont pour prendre du thé?

2.   Où est-ce qu'Amélie s'assoit?

Amélie **s'assoit** sur les marches du Château de la Princesse. Elle ne sait vraiment pas quoi faire. Au-dessus d'elle, il y a une grande image de la princesse. Amélie est si triste qu'elle ne s'aperçoit même pas de l'image.

Qu'est-ce que je dois faire?

Tu t'assois là et je m'assois ici.
You sit there and I sit here.

Nouveaux verbes
New Verbs

rentrer : *to go back*

retrouver : *to find again*

s'asseoir : *to sit*

Soudainement, la princesse sort de l'image et devient une vraie princesse **devant les yeux** d'Amélie. La princesse va vers Amélie qui est si enchantée qu'elle ne peut pas bouger.

« Bonjour Amélie! Aujourd'hui tu es allée sur un manège. Veux-tu essayer d'autres? » la princesse lui demande.

Réponses courtes

1. D'où est-ce que la princesse vient?

2. Qui accompagne Amélie sur le manège la Danse des Sirènes?

Amélie est la fille **la plus chanceuse**! Elle dit à la princesse qu'elle veut aller sur la Danse des Sirènes et voilà qu'elle est dans le manège!

Une sirène l'accompagne et elles **crient de joie** ensemble.

Ensuite elle va sur la Grande Ourse et cette fois c'est Capitaine Courageux qui l'accompagne! C'est encore plus amusant que la Danse des Sirènes!

Félicitations! Tu es la concurrente la plus chanceuse!

Congratulations! You are the luckiest contestant.

Nouvelles expressions
New Expressions

devant les yeux : before the eyes
la plus chanceuse : the luckiest
crier de joie : scream/shout with joy

Après, la princesse décide de l'amener au Grand Carrousel où Amélie **choisit** un joli cheval blanc qui **sourit**. La princesse regarde Amélie s'amuser et les deux sourient.

Elle tourne et tourne sans arrêt sur le manège le plus lumineux, les Ailes des Fées. Il y a même des fées qui **volent** autour d'Amélie.

Réponses courtes

1. Est-ce que la princesse l'accompagne sur le Grand Carrousel?

2. Qu'est-ce qu'Amélie fait au Château de la Princesse?

Ensuite Amélie prend du thé et des goûters au château avec la princesse et ses invités spéciaux. Ils parlent tous de leur journée et Amélie ne peut pas décider son moment préféré. Après cette journée amusante, Amélie est vraiment fatiguée. Elle commence à s'endormir et à faire des beaux rêves.

Nouveaux verbes
New Verbs

choisir : to choose

sourire : to smile   *voler : to fly*

s'apercevoir p.175 *: to notice*

« Réveille-toi, Amélie! Il est temps d'aller à la maison », lui dit son père. La voix de son père est si douce qu'Amélie ne sait pas si c'est réelle.

Est-ce que j'ai fait un rêve?

Elle ouvre ses yeux et elle se trouve dans le café avec ses parents. Elle regarde ses parents qui lui sourient. « Pourquoi souriez-vous comme ça? » elle leur demande.

Réponses courtes

1. **Qui réveille Amélie?**

2. **Est-ce qu'Amélie pense qu'elle fait un rêve?**

C'est le temps de retourner à la maison. Quand ils passent par le Château de la Princesse, Amélie regarde l'image de la princesse.

La princesse lui fait un clin d'œil! « Ouah, c'était réel! » pense Amélie avec une grande joie.

Merci pour une journée merveilleuse, Princesse!

Coin de grammaire
Grammar Corner

On utilise *le futur proche* pour exprimer une intention, une action ou un événement dans un futur proche.

On forme le futur proche avec le verbe « aller » conjugué au présent et l'infinitif du prochain verbe.

Amélie **va** **aller**
au présent l'infinitif
au parc d'attractions.

Est-ce que tu te rappelles?

Remplis les espaces pour compléter les phrases. Ensuite mets les événements en ordre.

Fill in the blanks to complete the sentences. Then put the events in order.

A. Amélie va aller au parc d'attractions avec ses parents mais elle peut seulement aller sur un _____ .

manège	autres
prend	yeux
rêve	sourit

B. Amélie _____ du thé avec la princesse et Amélie ne peut pas décider son moment préféré de la journée.

C. Ils vont prendre une petite pause au café où Amélie s'endort et fait un _____ qu'elle est enfermée dans le parc.

D. Amélie pense qu'elle a fait un rêve mais quand elle passe par le Château de la Princesse, elle regarde la princesse qui lui _____ .

E. Amélie s'endort encore et quand elle ouvre ses _____ elle est dans le café avec ses parents.

F.

Bonjour Amélie! Aujourd'hui tu es allée sur un manège. Veux-tu essayer d'_____ ?

Ordre d'événements

Corrige les erreurs

Corrige les erreurs d'orthographe, de conjugaison et de ponctuation dans le paragraphe suivant.

Correct the spelling, conjugation, and punctuation errors in the following paragraph.

Il y a 20 erreurs en total!

Une samedi matin, Amélie vont aller avec ses parent aux parc d'attractions. Elle sais que ses parents n'a pas asez d'argent et qu'elle peux seulment alle sur un manege Elle choisis la Maison Hantée et ils s'amuse beaucoup. Ensuite ils vont au cafe pour prendre du the et elle s'endors.

Elle fait un rêve ou la princesse l'amène sur tous les manège et ensuit elle se réveille au café avec ses parents.

Conjuguons ensemble

Complète les conjugaisons. Ensuite remplis les espaces avec la bonne conjugaison en utilisant « passer » ou « sourire ».

Complete the conjugations. Then fill in the blanks with the correct conjugation using "to pass" or "to smile".

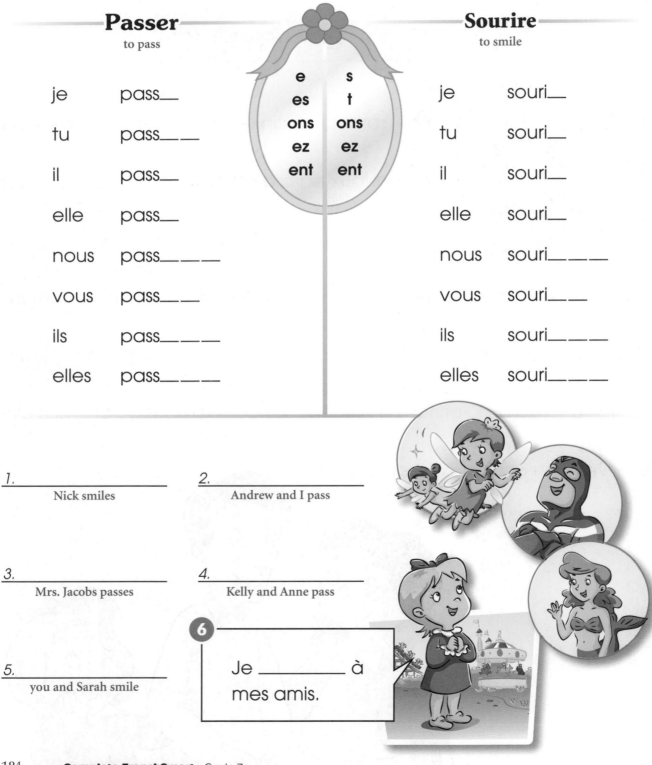

Passer
to pass

je	pass__
tu	pass___
il	pass__
elle	pass__
nous	pass____
vous	pass___
ils	pass____
elles	pass____

e   s
es   t
ons   ons
ez   ez
ent   ent

Sourire
to smile

je	souri__
tu	souri__
il	souri__
elle	souri__
nous	souri____
vous	souri___
ils	souri____
elles	souri____

1. _____
   Nick smiles

2. _____
   Andrew and I pass

3. _____
   Mrs. Jacobs passes

4. _____
   Kelly and Anne pass

5. _____
   you and Sarah smile

6 Je _____ à mes amis.

Conjuguons ensemble

Remplis les espaces à l'aide du tableau sur la page de gauche.
Fill in the blanks with the help of the table on the left page.

1. Sur le Grand Carrousel, le cheval qu'Amélie choisit lui _____ .

2. Amélie et la princesse s'amusent beaucoup ensemble et les deux _____ .

3. Elle _____ par le Château de la Princesse et elle veut entrer là aussi.

4. « Est-ce que nous _____ par la Maison Hantée? » elle demande à ses parents.

5. Quand le train entre dans le tunnel, ils _____ par des fantômes et des monstres.

6

Pourquoi est-ce que tu _____ quand elle _____ près de toi?

Résumé de l'histoire

Fais un résumé de l'histoire « La journée d'Amélie au parc d'attractions » à l'aide de la phrase et des mots donnés.

Summarize the story "Amelia's Day at the Theme Park" with the help of the given sentence and words.

La journée d'Amélie au parc d'attractions

| un manège |
| s'endormir |
| choisir |
| un rêve |
| se perdre |
| la journée |

Amélie est si enthousiaste parce qu'elle va aller au

parc d'attractions avec ses parents. _____

_____

_____

_____

_____

_____

Diamants et crapauds

Personnages

la jeune fille

la mère et la sœur aînée

la vieille femme

Il était une fois une jeune fille qui vivait avec sa mère et sa sœur **aînée**. Sa sœur était la préférée de sa mère car les deux étaient paresseuses et très difficiles avec tout le monde.

Maman, j'ai des fleurs pour vous.

Un jour, la jeune fille cueille un petit bouquet de fleurs pour sa mère et sa sœur. Mais elles reçoivent le cadeau **avec mépris**.

Réponses courtes

1. Qui est la fille préférée de la mère?

2. Est-ce que la jeune fille est paresseuse et difficile?

Au contraire de sa mère et de sa sœur, la jeune fille est très travailleuse et gentille. Elle n'est **pas du tout** paresseuse comme elles. C'est elle qui fait toutes les tâches ménagères à la maison. C'est elle qui nettoie la maison, c'est elle qui cuisine, c'est elle qui fait tout en fait!

Qu'est-ce qui te prend si longtemps?

Je suis ton frère aîné.
I am your elder brother.

Nouvelles expressions
New Expressions

aîné(e) : elder
avec mépris : with scorn
pas du tout : not at all

Chaque jour, la jeune fille marche pendant des heures pour chercher de l'eau d'un puits. Un jour, il y a une vieille femme assise près du puits. « J'ai tellement soif, est-ce que tu peux me donner un peu d'eau à boire? » elle demande à la jeune fille.

Voilà.

Tout de suite, la fille **remplit** son pichet et elle donne à boire à la vieille femme. La jeune fille est contente de pouvoir aider quelqu'un.

Réponses courtes

1. Qu'est-ce que la jeune fille fait chaque jour?

2. Pourquoi est-ce que la vieille femme lui donne un cadeau?

La vieille femme **révèle** qu'elle est en fait une bonne fée. Elle fait un geste de la main et dit à la jeune fille : « Tu es une fille généreuse et gentille et je veux te donner un cadeau pour te **remercier**. »

Quand la jeune fille **ouvre** la bouche pour lui remercier, une rose et deux perles tombent de sa bouche.

Nouveaux verbes
New Verbs

Ouvre la boîte pour voir ce qui est à l'intérieur.
Open the box to see what is inside.

remplir : to fill

révéler : to reveal

remercier : to thank   ouvrir : to open

La jeune fille ne sait pas quoi faire car elle ne peut pas ouvrir sa bouche sans avoir des roses, des perles et des diamants qui tombent. Elle court rapidement à la maison et raconte ce qui s'est passé à sa mère et à sa sœur.

Quand elle raconte l'histoire, des diamants et des perles tombent de sa bouche **comme des gouttes d'eau**.

Réponses courtes

1. Qu'est-ce qui tombe de la bouche de la jeune fille?

2. Qu'est-ce que la mère dit à sa fille aînée de faire?

La mère est **non seulement** paresseuse et difficile mais avide aussi. Elle veut avoir le même cadeau pour sa fille aînée et pense à un plan.

> Demain, tu vas aller au puits comme ta sœur le fait. La vieille femme va sûrement te donner un meilleur cadeau qu'elle.

Le lendemain, la fille aînée va au puits pour trouver la vieille femme. Elle espère recevoir **le même** cadeau que sa sœur.

> **Nous sommes les mêmes!**
> We are the same!

Nouvelles expressions
New Expressions

comme des gouttes d'eau : like drops of water

non seulement : not only

le même : the same

Après un long chemin, la fille aînée est fatiguée et très **fâchée**. Elle s'approche du puits et voit tout de suite une femme riche **assise** près du puits. La femme riche lui demande un peu d'eau à boire.

« Cette femme n'est pas la bonne fée que je cherche », pense la fille aînée et décide qu'elle ne va pas aider la femme riche.

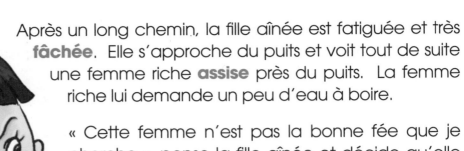

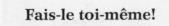
Fais-le toi-même!

Réponses courtes

1. Qui est la femme riche assise près du puits?

2. Est-ce que la fille aînée reçoit le même cadeau que sa sœur?

Soudainement, la femme riche se transforme en bonne fée.

> Je suis la bonne fée que tu cherches.

« Tu es une fille si **impolie**, méchante et pas généreuse du tout. Je vais te donner un cadeau mais ton cadeau va être très différent de celui de ta sœur », lui dit la bonne fée.

La fille aînée a si peur qu'elle commence à courir à la maison le plus vite possible.

> Pourquoi es-tu fâchée?
> Why are you angry?

Nouveaux mots
New Words

fâché(e) : angry

assis(e) : seated

impoli(e) : rude

Quand la fille aînée arrive à la maison, elle essaie de raconter à sa mère et à sa sœur ce qui s'est passé mais elle ne peut pas. Des crapauds et des serpents sortent de sa bouche. Sa sœur est très choquée et triste pour elle et **ressent** sa douleur.

Maman, aide-moi!

Réponses courtes

1. Qu'est-ce qui sort de la bouche de la fille aînée comme « cadeau »?

2. Pourquoi est-ce que la jeune fille part de la maison?

Sa mère est furieuse avec la jeune fille. Elle la **blâme** pour tout ce qui arrive à la fille aînée.

Tu n'es plus ma fille. Pars très loin et ne **reviens** jamais.

La jeune fille est très triste mais elle part tout de suite comme lui demande sa mère.

Ils me blâment pour le désordre.
They blame me for the mess.

Nouveaux verbes
New Verbs

ressentir : to feel

blâmer : to blame

revenir : to come back

La jeune fille marche dans la forêt et pleure sans pouvoir s'arrêter. Elle laisse derrière elle des perles, des roses et des diamants.

D'où viennent tous ces diamants?

Un prince voyage sur le même chemin que la fille et il voit le chemin qui brille. Il ne peut pas croire ses yeux et il commence à suivre la piste des bijoux jusqu'à la jeune fille.

Réponses courtes

1. Comment est-ce que le prince trouve la jeune fille?

2. Qu'est-ce que c'est la fin de cette histoire?

Quand le prince rencontre la jeune fille, il voit qu'elle est gentille et généreuse. La jeune fille aussi peut voir que le prince est un jeune homme noble et juste. Il lui demande ce qu'elle fait dans la forêt toute seule et elle lui raconte ce qui s'est passé avec sa mère.

Les deux tombent amoureux et se marient dans le royaume du prince. Jusqu'à ce jour, ils vivent encore heureux ensemble.

Elle <u>espère</u> <u>recevoir</u> le même cadeau.
verbe conjugué   l'infinitif

Coin de grammaire
Grammar Corner

Elle <u>essaie</u> <u>de</u> <u>raconter</u> à sa mère.
verbe conjugué ↑   l'infinitif
          préposition

Quand il y a deux verbes, un après l'autre, le premier se conjugue et le deuxième reste toujours à l'infinitif.

Parfois il y a des prépositions entre les deux.

Est-ce que tu te rappelles?

Remplis les espaces pour compléter les phrases. Ensuite mets les événements en ordre.

Fill in the blanks to complete the sentences. Then put the events in order.

A. Quand la jeune fille ouvre la bouche, des perles, des roses et des diamants _____ .

B. Un jeune prince la trouve dans la forêt et les deux tombent _____ , se marient et vivent heureux ensemble.

C. Une jeune fille habite avec sa mère et sa sœur _____ qui ne l'apprécient pas et elle fait tout le travail à la maison.

D. La mère est si fâchée que des crapauds et des serpents tombent de la bouche de la fille aînée qu'elle dit à la jeune fille de _____ .

E. Un jour, quand la jeune fille va au _____ , elle rencontre une bonne fée qui lui donne un beau cadeau .

F. La fille aînée va au puits mais elle est impolie et _____ et la bonne fée lui donne un cadeau différent.

amoureux
tombent
méchante
partir
aînée
puits

Ordre d'événements

☐ ☐ ☐ ☐ ☐ ☐

Qui a dit quoi?

Quels personnages de l'histoire ont dit les phrases suivantes? Relie la phrase au personnage qui correspond.

Which characters from the story said the following sentences? Match the sentence with the corresponding character.

A. « Bien sûr, je vais vous donner de l'eau à boire gentille vieille femme. »

B. « Qu'est-ce que tu fais toute seule dans la forêt…Veux-tu te marier avec moi? »

C. « Pars très loin et ne reviens jamais ici car tu n'es plus ma famille et ce n'est plus ta maison. »

D. « Tu es une fille généreuse et gentille. Pour ton aide, je veux te donner un cadeau pour te remercier. »

E. « Je veux le même cadeau car je veux avoir des perles et des diamants qui tombent de ma bouche. »

Conjuguons ensemble

Complète les conjugaisons. Ensuite remplis les espaces avec la bonne conjugaison en utilisant « tomber » ou « ouvrir ».

Complete the conjugations. Then fill in the blanks with the correct conjugation using "to fall" or "to open".

Tomber
to fall

je	tomb__
tu	tomb___
il	tomb__
elle	tomb__
nous	tomb_____
vous	tomb___
ils	tomb____
elles	tomb____

e
es
ons
ez
ent

Ouvrir
to open

j'	ouvr__
tu	ouvr___
il	ouvr__
elle	ouvr__
nous	ouvr_____
vous	ouvr___
ils	ouvr____
elles	ouvr____

1. _____
   Felicity and Ann open

2. _____
   Mike and I fall

3. _____
   Mrs. Doyle falls

4. _____
   you fall

5. _____
   she opens

6. _____
   Tom and Simon open

7. _____
   Tucker and Clara fall

8 _____

Quand j'_____ ma bouche, il y a des perles.

Conjuguons ensemble

Remplis les espaces à l'aide du tableau sur la page de gauche.
Fill in the blanks with the help of the table on the left page.

1.   Quand la jeune fille _____ la bouche pour lui remercier, une rose et deux perles tombent de sa bouche.

2.   « J'_____ ma bouche pour parler mais je ne peux pas! » la fille aînée dit.

3.   « Est-ce que tu _____ amoureuse? » demande le jeune prince à la jeune fille.

4.   « Si nous _____ amoureux tu vas être mon prince pour toujours », elle lui répond.

5.   Quand la fille aînée ouvre la bouche, des crapauds _____ .

6

Dépêchez-vous!
Je _____ !

7

Nous _____ le filet!

Résumé de l'histoire

Fais un résumé de l'histoire « Diamants et crapauds » à l'aide de la phrase et des mots donnés.

Summarize the story "Diamonds and Toads" with the help of the given sentence and words.

assise

un cadeau

la bonne fée

raconter

la bouche

amoureux

Une jeune fille vivait avec sa mère and sa sœur aînée. Un jour, _____

_____

_____

_____

_____

_____

_____

_____

Amusez-vous avec les dialogues

Have Fun with Dialogues

1. Make your conjugation book.

   a. Cut out pages 209 to 212.

   b. Cut along the dotted lines to make six spread pages.

   c. Fold the spread pages and put them in order.

   d. Staple them.

2. Complete the dialogues on page 207 with the help of the conjugation book. Then copy the correct dialogues in the boxes.

3. Write a short paragraph on page 208 to describe the picture with the help of the given words.

Amusons-nous dehors!
Let's Have Fun Outside!

Je _____ goûter le gâteau.
  to want

_____ à ta cage, mon oiseau.
to come back

Regarde-les, Teddy. C'_____
                          to be

tellement amusant!

Je _____ qu'ils _____
    to think   to be

incroyables aussi!

_____ les boutons maintenant!
to plant

Je _____ des livres au sujet des
   to read

ours. Ils _____ des animaux
            to be

incroyables!

L'oiseau _____ juste à temps!
          to arrive

_____ avec nous.
to eat

Je _____ que nous _____
   to believe   to be able to

être des jardiniers!

Je _____ des livres au sujet des
   to read

tigres. Ils _____ des animaux
             to be

effrayants!

_____ les graines maintenant.
to plant

Amusons-nous dehors!
Let's Have Fun Outside!

le chien

l'oiseau

la cage

les assiettes

le livre

Les ours

les graines

C'est une belle journée pour s'amuser dehors. _____

_____

_____

_____

_____

_____

_____

_____

Mon livre de **Conjugaison**

My Conjugation Book

	couvrir to cover	**dire** to say
je	couvre	dis
tu	couvres	dis
il	couvre	dit
elle	couvre	dit
nous	couvrons	disons
vous	couvrez	dites
ils	couvrent	disent
elles	couvrent	disent

21

	avoir to have
j'	ai
tu	as
il	a
elle	a
nous	avons
vous	avez
ils	ont
elles	ont

2

	venir to come	**convaincre** to convince
je	viens	convaincs
tu	viens	convaincs
il	vient	convainc
elle	vient	convainc
nous	venons	convainquons
vous	venez	convainquez
ils	viennent	convainquent
elles	viennent	convainquent

19

Tu manges mon poisson!

4

	être to be	**faire** to do
je	suis	fais
tu	es	fais
il	est	fait
elle	est	fait
nous	sommes	faisons
vous	êtes	faites
ils	sont	font
elles	sont	font

1

22

	planter to plant	**manger** to eat
je	plante	mange
tu	plantes	manges
il	plante	mange
elle	plante	mange
nous	plantons	mangeons
vous	plantez	mangez
ils	plantent	mangent
elles	plantent	mangent

3

	sortir to go out	**découvrir** to discover
	sors	découvre
	sors	découvres
	sort	découvre
	sort	découvre
	sortons	découvrons
	sortez	découvrez
	sortent	découvrent
	sortent	découvrent

20

	arrêter to stop	**envoyer** to send
j'	arrête	envoie
tu	arrêtes	envoies
il	arrête	envoie
elle	arrête	envoie
nous	arrêtons	envoyons
vous	arrêtez	envoyez
ils	arrêtent	envoient
elles	arrêtent	envoient

5

18

	pouvoir to be able to	croire to believe
je	peux	crois
tu	peux	crois
il	peut	croit
elle	peut	croit
nous	pouvons	croyons
vous	pouvez	croyez
ils	peuvent	croient
elles	peuvent	croient

17

	trouver to find	penser to think
	trouve	pense
	trouves	penses
	trouve	pense
	trouve	pense
	trouvons	pensons
	trouvez	pensez
	trouvent	pensent
	trouvent	pensent

6

	lire to read	vouloir to want
je	lis	veux
tu	lis	veux
il	lit	veut
elle	lit	veut
nous	lisons	voulons
vous	lisez	voulez
ils	lisent	veulent
elles	lisent	veulent

15

Elle touche le cactus.

8

	sauver to save	se moquer to make fun
je	sauve	me moque
tu	sauves	te moques
il	sauve	se moque
elle	sauve	se moque
nous	sauvons	nous moquons
vous	sauvez	vous moquez
ils	sauvent	se moquent
elles	sauvent	se moquent

13

	arriver to arrive
j'	arrive
tu	arrives
il	arrive
elle	arrive
nous	arrivons
vous	arrivez
ils	arrivent
elles	arrivent

J'arrive!

10

	toucher to touch	**passer** to pass
je	touche	passe
tu	touches	passes
il	touche	passe
elle	touche	passe
nous	touchons	passons
vous	touchez	passez
ils	touchent	passent
elles	touchent	passent

7

	revenir to come back
	reviens
	reviens
	revient
	revient
	revenons
	revenez
	reviennent
	reviennent

Reviens!

16

	se réveiller to wake up
je	me réveille
tu	te réveilles
il	se réveille
elle	se réveille
nous	nous réveillons
vous	vous réveillez
ils	se réveillent
elles	se réveillent

9

	réussir to succeed	**finir** to finish
	réussis	finis
	réussis	finis
	réussit	finit
	réussit	finit
	réussissons	finissons
	réussissez	finissez
	réussissent	finissent
	réussissent	finissent

14

	jouer to play	**pousser** to grow
je	joue	pousse
tu	joues	pousses
il	joue	pousse
elle	joue	pousse
nous	jouons	poussons
vous	jouez	poussez
ils	jouent	poussent
elles	jouent	poussent

11

	respirer to breathe
	respire
	respires
	respire
	respire
	respirons
	respirez
	respirent
	respirent

Nous respirons...

12

Réponses Answers

1 Les sports
Sports

B. A: Quand il neige, j'aime aller à la montagne.
    B: Quand je fais du ski je prends le télésiège.
    C: Quand je fais du canotage je porte un gilet de sauvetage.
    D: Je fais du parachutisme.
    E: Je joue au soccer avec un ballon de football.

C. 1. J'ai besoin d'une raquette de tennis pour jouer au tennis.
    2. J'ai besoin d'un costume de bain pour faire de la natation.
    3. J'ai besoin d'un canot pour faire du canotage.

D. 1. font du ski
    2. fait de l'alpinisme
    3. font de la planche à neige
    4. joue au soccer
    5. jouons au hockey
    6. faisons du canotage
    7. fais de la plongée sous-marine
    8. jouez au tennis

E. 1. sud-ouest
    2. L'hôpital est à l'est de moi.
    3. L'aéroport est à l'ouest de moi.
    4. Le restaurant est au nord-ouest de moi.
    5. Les toilettes sont au sud-est de moi.
    6. Le parking est au sud de moi.

F. 1. à gauche de
    2. à droite de
    3. à droite de ; à gauche de
    4. tout droit ; à droite
    5. tout droit ; à sa droite ; tout droit

2 La vie marine
Marine Life

A. 1. le calmar
    2. la pastenague
    3. le crabe
    4. la baleine
    5. l'étoile de mer
    6. le dauphin
    7. le requin
    8. le homard
    9. la tortue de mer
    10. l'éponge de mer
    11. les algues
    12. la méduse
    13. la pieuvre

B. Ils ont des tentacules :
    le calmar ; la pieuvre ; la méduse
    Ils ont une carapace :
    la tortue de mer ; le homard ; le crabe
    Ils ont des nageoires :
    le dauphin ; le requin ; la baleine

C. la pieuvre : octopus
    le homard : lobster
    le dauphin : dolphin
    les algues : seaweed
    la pastenague : stingray

D. 1. italienne   2. belle
    3. molles   4. frais
    5. gros   6. douce
    7. beaux   8. gentille

E. grand ; ancien ; blanche ; grises ; sombre ; profond ; blancs ; doux ; sèches ; mouillées ; gros ; délicieux ; délicats ; frais

F. 1. Je mange beaucoup de légumes **frais**.
    2. Elles portent des jupes **courtes**.
    3. Nous portons de **nouveaux** chandails de hockey.
    4. Mon **vieux** chien n'aime plus courir dans le parc.
    5. La **jolie** robe est dans le **petit** magasin.
    6. Ils vont bâtir un **nouvel** hôtel à côté du **petit** pont.

G. A: grande
    B: Le requin est cruel, il n'est pas gentil.
    C: Le crabe est premier, il n'est pas dernier.
    D: Les algues sont longues, elles ne sont pas courtes.

H. 1. plus ; que
    2. moins drôle que
    3. plus grande que
    4. moins joli que
    5. plus vieille que

Complete FrenchSmart · Grade 7   213

3 L'impératif
The Imperative

B. 1. finis 2. mangeons
3. rends 4. réussissez
5. sautent 6. obéissent
7. réponds 8. remplis
9. parle 10. défend

C. Répondez à la questions! : C
Lave-toi! : A
Choisis un livre! : A
Finissons le cours! : B
Écoutons les annonces! : B

D. 1. Finis 2. Lave
3. Nourris 4. Rends
5. Mange 6. Chantez
7. Répondez 8. Choisissez
9. Vendons 10. Finissons
11. Remplissez

E. 1. Ne lave pas mon chandail à la machine!
2. Ne nageons jamais dans le lac!
3. Ne jouez jamais au football américain sans casques!
4. Ne mange plus de bonbons!

F. 1. Arrête de parler!
2. Arrêtons d'étudier!
3. Arrête de sauter sur ton lit!
4. Arrêtez de nager dans la piscine!
5. Arrêtez de salir vos robes!
6. Arrête de marcher sur le canapé!
7. Arrêtez d'écouter aux portes!

4 La technologie et l'Internet
Technology and the Internet

B. 1. tape ; le clavier
2. surfe ; l'Internet
3. clique ; l'icône
4. tapez
5. envoie ; un courriel

C. 1. L'étudiant, a-t-il besoin d'aide?
2. Cherchons-nous le mot clé sur le site Web?
3. Son adresse électronique est-elle vjoor245@popular.com?
4. Zoé, télécharge-t-elle ses devoirs du site Web?

D. 1. Quel 2. Quel 3. Quelles
4. Quel 5. Quelle 6. Quels
7. Quel 8. Quelles

E. 1. Quel ; jérôme177@pop.world.ca.
2. Quelle ; L'adresse de la page d'accueil est www.popularbook.ca.
3. Quelle ; La couleur principale de la page est grise.
4. quelle ; Le curseur se trouve sur l'image du garçon.
5. Quel ; Le mot de passe de Jérôme est « populaire ».
6. quelle ; Jérôme envoie le courriel à mélodie333@pop.world.ca.

F. 1. Oui
2. Non, Jérôme n'est pas sur la page d'accueil.
3. Non, Jérôme ne clique pas sur l'icône de l'imprimante.
4. Oui, Jérôme envoie le message.
5. Oui, le garçon est à gauche du message.
6. Non, le mot de passe est « populaire ».
7. Oui, le sujet du message est « FrenchSmart est un vrai régal! ».
8. Non, Jérôme n'annule pas le message.

5 Le monde
The World

B.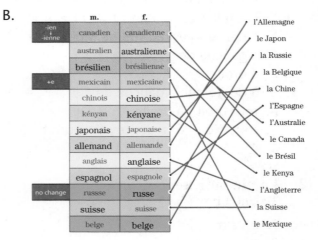

C. 1. au 2. en 3. en
4. au 5. en 6. aux
7. en 8. en 9. En

D. 1. en Suisse   2. en Corée du Sud
    3. au Canada   4. au Zimbabwe
    5. en Espagne   6. en France
    7. au Pérou   8. en Colombie
    9. en Angleterre   10. en Égypte

E. au ; en ; au ; en ; au ; en ; au
    1. Joseph-Armand Bombardier est né au Québec.
    2. Il est canadien.
    3. On les trouve en France, au Mexique, en Inde, au Japon, en Corée du Sud et au Canada.

6   Au jardin
In the Garden

B. 1. descends   2. jardin
    3. tondre   4. le gazon
    5. fais   6. arracher
    7. les fleurs   8. travailler
    9. planter   10. regarder
   11. cueillir   12. arroser
   13. remplir   14. arrosoir
   15. regarder   16. les vers
   17. la terre   18. le gazon
   19. pousser

C. 1. Est-ce que
    2. Est-ce que Manon pousse la brouette?
    3. Est-ce que nous arrosons le jardin?
    4. Est-ce que tu remplis l'arrosoir?
    5. Est-ce que tu portes des gants de jardinage?
    6. Est-ce que tu as faim Minou?

D. 1. Où   2. Combien de
    3. Où   4. Quand
    5. Comment   6. Qui
    7. Pourquoi

E. 1. objet ; Qu'est-ce que Marie mange?
    2. sujet ; Qui est-ce qui embrasse son chat?
    3. objet ; Qui est-ce que Paul aime?

F. 1. Combien de
    2. Quand est-ce que vous plantez vos graines?
    3. Où est votre jardin?
    4. Pourquoi est-ce que vous plantez toujours des roses?
    5. Comment est-ce que vous arrosez vos plantes?

    6. Comment est-ce que vous cueillez vos fleurs?

7   La fête
The Party

B.

C. 1. Nous allons à cette fête.
    2. Cet étudiant aime ce livre
    3. Ces hamburgers sont fantastiques.

D. 1. ce
    2. Cette photo est belle.
    3. Ce cadeau est grand.
    4. Ces bougies sont longues.
    5. Ces jeux sont amusants.
    6. Cette assiette est jetable.

E. 1. ci ; ces
    2. Cette ; ci ; cette
    3. ces ; ces ; là
    4. Ces ; ces ; ci
    5. ce ; ci
    6. ces ; ces ; là
    7. cette ; cette ; là

F. Cette ; ses ; ces ; sa ; ses ; son ; Cette ; cette ; ce ; ces ; Cette ; ce ; ces ; Cet ; Ce ; Cette

G. 1. This animal here is very pretty.
    2. These sunglasses are red.
    3. His/Her movies are longer than these movies here.
    4. That gift there is yours. Happy birthday!

H. 1. Cette tranche de pizza est à moi; celle-là est à toi.
    2. Ben veut ce cadeau-ci; Paul veut ce cadeau-là.
    3. Nous pouvons jouer cette musique-ci mais nous ne pouvons pas jouer cette musique-là.
    4. Je n'aime pas ces ballons-là; j'aime ces ballons-ci.
    5. Ces bonbons-ci sont à moi; ces bonbons-là sont à toi.

8 Quand? Où? Comment?
When? Where? How?

B. 1. souvent
    2. maintenant
    3. demain
    4. aujourd'hui
C. 1. Où ; partout/là
    2. Où ; ici ; là
    3. Où ; près
    4. Où ; là ; ici
D. 1. jouons ; ce
    2. Je mange seul.
    3. Le lapin saute vite.
    4. Nous dansons ensemble.
    5. Ça va mal.
    6. Je marche lentement.
    7. Le wagon descend vite!
E. 1. vais   2. ne vais pas aller
    3. mange   4. dînons
    5. danse   6. nageons
    7. va rendre   8. ne jouent jamais
F. 1. vais finir mes devoirs dans une heure
    2. vais arroser mon jardin dans un jour
    3. va partir dans une minute.
    4. allons prendre nos vacances dans une semaine.

14. jetables   15. croustilles
16. piles   17. prends
18. ici   19. le dernier
20. jamais
D. 2 ; 4 ; 1 ; 5 ; 6 ; 3
E. A: le télésiège   B: La méduse
    C: l'écran   D: piles
F. La voile est... : E
    L'Amérique du Nord est... : H
    Je remplis ma brouette... : A
    Dans mon jardin j'aime... : G
    On porte un gilet de sauvetage... : D
    Les étudiants bloguent... : J
    On joue des jeux vidéo... : F
    L'Afrique est... : C
    La Corée du Sud est... : I
    Le crabe a... : B
G. 1. le blogue   2. réussir
    3. le base-ball   4. le dauphin
    5. un Mexicain   6. la brouette
    7. cette boisson   8. les États-Unis
H. 1. sud   2. mal
    3. à l'eau   4. entendre
    5. hier   6. ouest
    7. vite   8. jamais
    9. loin   10. rarement

La révision 1
Revision 1

A. A: fait ; ski ; tuque
    B: Le requin ; nageoire
    C: Arrête ; salir ; faire
    D: tape ; clavier ; clique ; souris
    E: Le Canada ; un pays ; Amérique du Nord
    F: jardin ; tondons ; arrachons
    G: un gâteau ; la fête ; appareil photo
    H: toujours ; partout ; seul
B. 1. faux   2. vrai   3. vrai
    4. faux   5. faux   6. vrai
C. 1. au Mexique   2. Aujourd'hui
    3. la plongée sous-marine
    4. loin   5. bien
    6. sautons   7. nage
    8. Là   9. algues
    10. petit   11. nourris
    12. Maintenant   13. partout

9 Le magasinage
Shopping

B. 1. le pain ; la boulangerie
    2. le poulet ; la boucherie
    3. la laitue ; l'épicerie
    4. le tee-shirt ; la boutique
C. 1. tien
    2. C'est la mienne.
    3. Nous aimons la nôtre.
    4. Marie danse avec les siens.
    5. Vous allez à la vôtre.
    6. Tu embrasses le tien.
D. 1. le mien   2. la vôtre
    3. les leurs   4. la nôtre
    5. les siens   6. le vôtre/tien
E. 1. vôtre   2. le tien
    3. la mienne   4. les nôtres/la nôtre
    5. la mienne

F. 1. Combien coûte la baguette?
   Elle coûte deux dollars.
2. Combien coûtent les muffins?
   Ils coûtent six dollars.
3. Combien coûte la boîte de conserve?
   Elle coûte soixante-dix cents.
4. Combien coûte la pieuvre/le jouet?
   Elle/Il coûte quarante-cinq cents.

G. 1. Combien coûte une sucette?
   Une sucette coûte deux dollars.
   Combien coûtent trois sucettes?
   Trois sucettes coûtent cinq dollars.
2. Combine coûte l'avion rouge?
   Il coûte neuf dollars.
   Combien coûte l'avion bleu?
   Il coûte douze dollars.
3. Combien coûtent la blouse et la jupe?
   Elles coûtent quarante-quatre dollars.
   Combien coûte la robe?
   Elle coûte trente dollars.
   La robe est la plus chère.

10 Les verbes du 3ᵉ groupe
Verbs from the 3ʳᵈ Group

B. A: dormir   B: lire
   C: dire   D: écrire
   E: partir   F: sortir
C. 1. veut   2. savons   3. doit
   4. doit   5. Pouvez   6. dois
   7. devez
D. dorment ; sont ; sont ; Sortez ; dormez ;
   peuvent ; dormir ; sors ; Devons ; partir
E. 1. lit ; lisons
   2. dis ; dit
   3. conduit ; conduisez
   4. écris ; écris
   5. lisez ; lis
   6. disent ; disons
   7. écrivons
   8. conduisez
   9. lis ; écris
   10. dites
F. 2. devoir ; 1ʳᵉ ; pluriel
   3. dormir ; 2ᵉ ; singulier
   4. savoir ; 1ʳᵉ ; singulier
   5. dormir ; 3ᵉ ; singulier

6. vouloir ; 1ʳᵉ ; singulier
7. partir ; 2ᵉ ; singulier
8. devoir ; 2ᵉ ; singulier
9. conduire ; 3ᵉ ; singulier
10. partir ; 2ᵉ ; pluriel

11 Le journal
The Newspaper

B. A: Voyages/Monde
   B: Météo
   C: Cinéma
   D: Politique
   E: Sports
   F: Petites Annonces

C.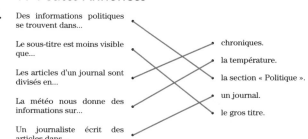

D. 1. La section « Société » va annoncer une grève.
   2. Nous allons lire la section « Météo » pour vérifier la température.
   3. Monsieur le Premier ministre va partir en France.
   4. Mon père va vouloir la section « Sports ».
   5. Marie va lire le journal chaque jour.
   6. Le journaliste va écrire un article sur la grève.

E. A: vais ; le journal
   B: La section « Politique » va annoncer le nouveau président.
   C: Ma mère et moi, allons lire la section « Monde ».
   D: Les garçons vont vouloir regarder un film.
   E: Tu va savoir la nouvelle.
   F: Ma famille va écrire une lettre à l'éditeur.
   G: Nous allons partir en Italie en avion.
   H: Il va vouloir regarder le jeu de soccer.

F. 1. Il ne va pas lire la section « Société ».
   2. Mes fleurs ne vont jamais vouloir de l'eau.
   3. Claudette et Thérèse ne vont plus pouvoir regarder un film.

4. Je ne vais pas aller au magasin à pied.
5. Zoé ne va pas écrire une lettre à ses parents.

G. 1. P   2. F   3. F
   4. P   5. F   6. P
   7. P   8. F

2. a. Annie et son frère ont deux-cent trente livres.
   b. Bernard a vingt-trois livres.
3. Il doit y mettre cent grammes de farine.
4. un ; cent
5. un ; mille

12 Les nombres : de 1 à 1000
Numbers: 1 to 1000

B. 1. trois ; sept   2. cent ; douze
   3. seize   4. six ; soixante-quatre
   5. cinq cent   6. cinquante-cinq
   7. 273   8. 434
   9. 718   10. 555
  11. 312

C. A: neuf cent vingt dollars
   B: quatre-vingt-six dollars
   C: sept cent soixante-huit dollars
   D: quatre-vingt-deux ; quarante
   E: cent trente-neuf dollars et soixante cents
   F: cinq dollars et quarante-cinq cents
   G: deux cent cinquante-trois dollars et quatre-vingt-quatre cents

D. 1. sept cent soixante-dix-sept
   2. six cent soixante
   3. quatre cent quatre-vingt-dix-sept
   4. neuf cent quatorze

E. A: 250 ; Mille sur quatre, ça fait deux cent cinquante.
   B: 694 ; Deux fois trois cent quarante-sept, ça fait six cent quatre-vingt-quatorze.
   C: 780 ; Deux cent soixante fois trois, ça fait sept cent quatre-vingts.
   D: 110 ; Cinq cent cinquante sur cinq, ça fait cent dix.
   E: 102 ; Six cent douze sur six, ça fait cent deux.
   F: 820 ; Dix fois quatre-vingt-deux, ça fait huit cent vingt.

F. 1. Jean et Marie ont assez d'enfants.
   2. En hiver, il y a trop de neige.
   3. Beaucoup de fleurs poussent dans son jardin.
   4. Il a peu d'argent pour acheter la bague.
   5. Elle boit beaucoup de boisson gazeuse.

G. 1. Sa mère a trente-sept ans.

13 Au musée
At the Museum

B. 1. remarquer   2. fascinante
   3. expose   4. historique
   5. veut toucher   6. le plan
   7. l'atelier   8. l'exposition
   9. précieuses

C. 1. two
   2. toucher₁ : *vt* (verbe transitif)
     meaning: to touch, to feel, to reach, to affect
    toucher₂ : *nm* (nom masculin)
     meaning: sense of touch

D. 1. peut toucher
   2. devons attendre
   3. peux guider
   4. veulent visiter
   5. dois passer
   6. pouvez regarder
   7. veux savoir
   8. savent garder

E. 1. Pouvez ; aller
   2. Peut-il faire ses devoirs?/Peux-tu faire tes devoirs?
   3. Peux-tu marcher plus vite?
   4. Pouvons-nous téléphoner à Marie?
   5. Pouvez-vous attendre mon frère?

F. La salle ; L'exposition ; Les heures d'ouverture ; va exposer ; œuvres ; pouvez observer ; pouvez visiter ; devez ; billets ; peuvent guider ; Visitez
   1. On peut voir les œuvres d'Emily Carr au Musée des beaux arts, en août.
   2. On peut observer les œuvres d'Emily Carr de près.
   3. Non, on peut visiter sa maison en regardant la projection du film « Emily Carr : la vie d'une artiste ».
   4. On doit acheter les billets en avance.

14 Les médias
The Media

B. 1. ses lecteurs.
   2. la radio.
   3. réseau.
   4. la télévision.
   5. presse écrite.
   6. informations.

C. 1. Je dois aller à l'école à pied.
   2. La CBC déclare être un réseau national.
   3. Vous voulez écrire aux écrivains de cet article.
   4. Ils pensent parler à leurs parents.

D. 1. Pense-t-elle être une bonne auditrice?
   2. Peut-il connecter les gens?
   3. Entends-tu parler les vieilles dames?
   4. Aime-t-il regarder les comédies de situation à la télévision?
   5. Dois-tu prendre le métro aujourd'hui?
   6. Allons-nous manger des pommes de terre?
   7. Avouent-ils être les amis de Paul?

E. 1. Nous ne devons pas avoir honte.
   2. Joseph et Sarah ne veulent plus annoncer la nouvelle.
   3. Qui est-ce qui ne pense jamais être beau?
   4. Tu ne peux guère communiquer avec tes parents sur l'Internet.

F. 1. B   2. A

G. Savez ; peut remplir ; dois avouer ; peuvent se connecter ; va remplacer ; veut dire ; pouvons

H. 1. 30 tonnes
   2. l'Internet
   3. (Réponses suggérées)
      L'Internet et la presse écrite./Les écoles virtuelles.

15 Le transport
Transportation

B. 1. les rails.   2. l'arrêt d'autobus.
   3. une voile.   4. un avion.

C. A: vais ; train/métro
   B: Tu vas à vélo.
   C: Nous allons en bateau.
   D: Ils vont en avion.
   E: Elle va à pied.

D. A: de ; l'école
   B: Nous descendons de l'école à la bibliothèque.
   C: Tu montes du restaurant à la maison.
   D: Elle va du parc au restaurant.
   E: Je reviens de Toronto à Montréal.
   F: Vous arrivez de Montréal à New York.

E. 1. viens
   2. viens du Canada.
   3. a. viennent du Maroc.
      b. vient du Maroc.
   4. a. venons de la France.
      b. vient de la France.
   5. a. venez de l'Angleterre.
      b. viennent de l'Angleterre.

F. 1. de ; à   2. à ; de
   3. à   4. à

G. 1. de   2. à   3. de
   4. d'   5. à   6. à
   7. de ; à 8. à

H. à ; en ; de ; à ; à ; au ; des ; des ; des ; à ; de ; au ; au ; à ; au
   1. Elle va à Paris.
   2. Elle rêve des croissants, des pains au chocolat et des tartes aux abricots.
   3. Elles boivent du chocolat chaud en attendant leurs croissants.

16 L'art et la culture
Art and Culture

B. 1. D   2. F   3. C
   4. E   5. B   6. A

C. 1. me   2. se   3. t' ; s'
   4. s'   5. nous   6. me
   7. nous

D. 1. Réveillons-nous tôt le matin!
   2. Sentez-vous contents!
   3. Habille-toi bien!
   4. Couche-toi de bonne heure!
   5. Promenons-nous dans la forêt!
   6. Couchez-vous!
   7. Lave-toi!

E. 1. You always entertain yourselves at the park.
      You always have fun at the park.
   2. The camel finds itself in the desert.
      The camel is found in the desert.

3. I stop myself in front of the subway station.
   I stop in front of the subway station.
4. We present ourselves to the teacher on the first day of school.
   We introduce ourselves to the teacher on the first day of school.

F. 1. Vous ne vous appelez pas Mme Leblanc.
   2. Je ne me réveille pas à 4 h.

G. se couche ; ne se réveille pas ; se rend ; s'habillent ; se sentent ; s'agit ; Dépêche ; ne se fâche pas ; se trouvent

On conduit... : F
Les musées exposent... : L
Les gâteaux sont... : K
Les spectateurs regardent... : I

G. 1. l'écrivain   2. lire
   3. trente-deux   4. le journal
   5. à cheval   6. le poète
   7. l'atelier   8. les gants

H. 1. 571   2. 310
   3. 1002   4. 237
   5. 916   6. 689
   7. 452   8. 764
   9. 122   10. 848

La révision 2
Revision 2

A. A: aller ; le dépanneur ; lait ; jus
   B: sors ; lis ; pars
   C: journal ; Dessins ; Météo
   D: assez ; soixante-cinq ; peu
   E: billets ; plan ; musée ; billetterie
   F: le gros titre ; journal
   G: autobus ; pied
   H: artiste ; peintures

B. 1. faux   2. faux   3. vrai
   4. faux   5. vrai   6. faux

C. 1. le journal   2. savoir
   3. voulons   4. à vélo
   5. Ma   6. avoue
   7. Culture   8. une exposition
   9. bien   10. remarquons
   11. pouvons   12. trop
   13. devons   14. observons
   15. baguette   16. soixante-quinze
   17. musée   18. Combien coûte
   19. touchez   20. passer

D. 2 ; 5 ; 6 ; 1 ; 3 ; 4

E. 1. B   2. C
   3. B   4. B

F. On dort... : E
   Nous voyageons... : G
   L'Internet est... : J
   La caissière travaille... : B
   La voiture coûte... : C
   Ils se lavent... : A
   Les nouvelles se trouvent... : H
   On écrit... : D

Histoire 1
Le cœur du singe

p. 128 Est-ce que tu te rappelles?

A: triste B: cœur
C: sur le dos D: crée
E: respirer F: se moquer

D ; C ; E ; B ; F ; A

p. 129 Corrige les erreurs

Dans la river̶ [ière] vit̶ [vent] deux crocodile(s) grand(s) et

méchant(s) qui croit̶ [ent] qu'ils vont manger le cœur [œu]
du sing(e). Le singe voient̶ [t] les crocodiles et

pensent̶ qu'ils est̶ [sont] gentil(s). Le crocodile crée̶n̶s̶ [e]

un plan pour dupe(r) le singe et le mange(r). Mais le

singe est plus sages̶ que les crocodiles et apprend

sa leçon qu'il ne peux̶ [t] pas faire confiance au(x)

crocodiles. À la fin, quand il voy̶o̶n̶s̶ [it] sa femme, il se

sent trist(e).

p. 130 Conjuguons ensemble

crée ; crées ; crée ; crée ; créons ; créez ; créent ;
créent
crois ; crois ; croit ; croit ; croyons ; croyez ;
croient ; croient

1. je crois 2. ils créent
3. elle crée 4. elle croit
5. vous créez 6. ils croient
7. nous créons 8. crois

p. 131 Conjuguons ensemble

1. croient 2. crée
3. créez 4. croit
5. croit 6. créons
7. crois

p. 132 Résumé de l'histoire
(Réponse individuelle)

Histoire 2
L'aventure du petit ânon

p. 146 Est-ce que tu te rappelles?

A: marché B: l'ânon
C: monter D: vendent
E: fermier F: villageois

A ; F ; C ; B ; E ; D

p. 147 Qui a dit quoi?

p. 148 Conjuguons ensemble

écoute ; écoutes ; écoute ; écoute ;
écoutons ; écoutez ; écoutent ; écoutent
entends ; entends ; entendons ; entendez ;
entendent ; entendent

1. elles entendent 2. elle écoute
3. vous écoutez 4. nous entendons
5. elle entend 6. ils écoutent
7. j'écoute 8. il entend
9. écoute

p. 149 Conjuguons ensemble

1. écoutent
2. entendent
3. écoute
4. écoutez
5. écoute
6. entends
7. entends ; (Réponse individuelle)

p. 150 Résumé de l'histoire
(Réponse individuelle)

Histoire 3
Une découverte près de la mer

p. 164 Est-ce que tu te rappelles?
A: ensoleillé   B: tourner
C: méchants   D: grotte
E: inoubliable   F: trésors
A ; D ; F ; C ; B ; E

p. 165 À l'écrit
A: Les enfants ont très peur et ne savent pas comment s'échapper.
B: Jeanne utilise les coquilles sur la plage pour décorer le château.
C: Charles est le premier à voir une grotte et il dit aux autres.
D: Tout d'un coup, des lumières brillantes éclairent la grotte.
E: Ils sont un peu tristes que l'expérience se finit.

p. 166 Conjuguons ensemble
donne ; donnes ; donne ; donne ; donnons ; donnez ; donnent ; donnent
commence; commences; commence; commence; commençons ; commencez ; commencent ; commencent
1. nous donnons   2. tu commences
3. il donne   4. vous commencez
5. ils donnent   6. ils commencent
7. donnes

p. 167 Conjuguons ensemble
1. donne   2. commencent
3. commence   4. donnent
5. commence   6. donne
7. commence

p. 168 Résumé de l'histoire
(Réponse individuelle)

Histoire 4
La journée d'Amélie au parc d'attractions

p. 182 Est-ce que tu te rappelles?
A: manège   B: prend
C: rêve   D: sourit
E: yeux   F: autres
A ; C ; F ; B ; E ; D

p. 183 Corrige les erreurs

Une̶ samedi matin, Amélie v̶o̶n̶t̶ [va] aller avec ses parent[s] aux̶ parc d'attractions. Elle sai[t] que ses parents n'e̶ [ont] pas a[s]ez d'argent et qu'elle peu[t] seul[e]ment alle[r] sur un manège. Elle choisi[t] la Maison Hantée et ils s'amuse[nt] beaucoup. Ensuite ils vont au café pour prendre du thé et elle s'endor[t]. Elle fait un rêve où la Princesse l'amène sur tous les manège[s] et ensuit[e] elle se réveille au café avec ses parents.

p. 184 Conjuguons ensemble
passe ; passes ; passe ; passe ; passons ; passez ; passent ; passent
souris ; souris ; sourit ; sourit ; sourions ; souriez ; sourient ; sourient
1. il sourit   2. nous passons
3. elle passe   4. elles passent
5. vous souriez   6. souris

p. 185 Conjuguons ensemble
1. sourit   2. sourient
3. passe   4. passons
5. passent   6. souris ; passe

p. 186 Résumé de l'histoire
(Réponse individuelle)

Histoire 5
Diamants et crapauds

p. 200 Est-ce que tu te rappelles?
A: tombent   B: amoureux
C: aînée   D: partir
E: puits   F: méchante
C ; E ; A ; F ; D ; B

p. 201 Qui a dit quoi?

p. 202　Conjuguons ensemble

tombe ; tombes ; tombe ; tombe ; tombons ;
tombez ; tombent ; tombent

ouvre ; ouvres ; ouvre ; ouvre ; ouvrons ; ouvrez ;
ouvrent ; ouvrent

1. elles ouvrent
2. nous tombons
3. elle tombe
4. tu tombes
5. elle ouvre
6. ils ouvrent
7. ils tombent
8. ouvre

p. 203　Conjuguons ensemble

1. ouvre
2. ouvre
3. tombes
4. tombons
5. tombent
6. tombe
7. ouvrons

p. 204　Résumé de l'histoire

(Réponse individuelle)

Amusez-vous avec les dialogues
Have Fun with Dialogues

p. 208　Amusons-nous dehors!
　　　　　Let's Have Fun Outside!

(Écriture individuelle)

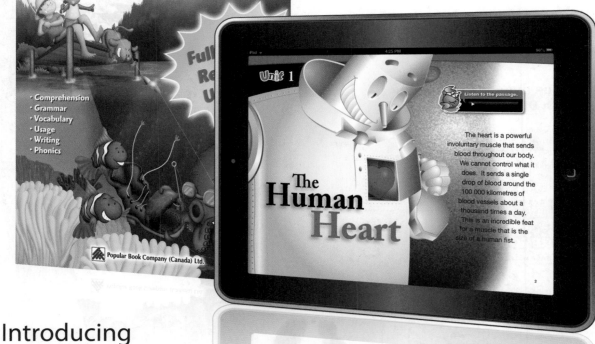

ideals
TRAVEL

There's a call in my heart for the great outdoors;
There's a longing within my breast
To seek the depths of the deepest woods,
Where I find, in their solitude, rest.

There's a charm in the great outdoors for me,
In the music of birds and breeze,
In the soughing pines and the swishing boughs,
The voice and the cry of the trees.

There is ever within me a strong desire
To gaze on the restless sea;
And its rolling waves, and its noisy roar,
Are a soothing tonic to me.

There's a yearning to wander in desert sands;
To pass away lightly the hours,
To inhale the dry air and to feast tired eyes,
On the patches of gay-colored flowers.

There's a cry in my soul of thankfulness,
That I am permitted to see,
To hear and to feel the touch of God,
In the wonders of land and sea.

Agnes Davenport Bond

Publisher, James A. Kuse
Managing Editor, Ralph Luedtke
Editor/Ideals, Colleen Callahan Gonring
Associate Editor, Linda Robinson
Production Manager, Mark Brunner
Photographic Editor, Gerald Koser
Copy Editor, Norma Barnes
Art Editor, Duane Weaver
Contributing Editor, Beverly Wiersum Charette

ISBN 0-89542-333-2

IDEALS—Vol. 37, No. 5 July MCMLXXX. IDEALS (ISSN 0019-137X) is published eight times a year,
January, February, April, June, July, September, October, November
by IDEALS PUBLISHING CORPORATION, 11315 Watertown Plank Road, Milwaukee, Wis. 53201
Second class postage paid at Milwaukee, Wisconsin. Copyright © MCMLXXX by IDEALS PUBLISHING CORPORATION.
All rights reserved. Title IDEALS registered U.S. Patent Office.
Published Simultaneously in Canada.

ONE YEAR SUBSCRIPTION—eight consecutive issues as published—only $15.95
TWO YEAR SUBSCRIPTION—sixteen consecutive issues as published—only $27.95
SINGLE ISSUES—only $2.95

Windmills

The most foreign and picturesque structures on the Cape, to an inlander, not excepting the saltworks, are the windmills—gray-looking, octagonal towers, with long timbers slanting to the ground in the rear, and there resting on a cartwheel, by which their fans are turned round to face the wind. These appeared also to serve in some measure for props against its force. A great circular rut was worn around the building by the wheel. [The windmills] looked loose and slightly locomotive, like huge wounded birds, trailing a wing or a leg, and reminded one of pictures of the Netherlands.

Being on elevated ground, and high in themselves, they serve as landmarks, for there are no tall trees, or other objects commonly, which can be seen at a distance in the horizon; though the outline of the land itself is so firm and distinct, that an insignificant cone, or even precipice of sand, is visible at a great distance from over the sea. Sailors making the land commonly steer either by the windmills, or the meetinghouses. In the country, we are obliged to steer by the meetinghouses alone. Yet the meeting-house is a kind of windmill, which runs one day in seven, turned either by the winds of doctrine or public opinion, or more rarely by the winds of Heaven, where another sort of grist is ground, of which, if it be not all bran or musty, if it be not *plaster*, we trust to make bread of life.

Henry David Thoreau

Robert Louis Stevenson

As a young boy, Robert Louis Stevenson dreamed of becoming a "man of letters," and made a vow early in life that he would learn to write. An only child who possessed a weak disposition and frail body, Stevenson spent most of his youth playing in a fantasy world populated by the adventurous, robust heroes of childhood fables. These stories of his childhood took the lonely, sensitive boy out of himself, as in later years the Scottish author would take countless other children and adults on the same magical flights of fancy. A collection of poems recalling his boyhood experiences are contained in the volume, *A Child's Garden of Verses*, especially in the set subtitled, "The Child Alone." According to his father's wishes, Stevenson was sent to Edinburgh University to study law, but the budding author devoted more time to writing and editing a university magazine than to his studies. After his schooling, Stevenson traveled to France where he met Fanny Osbourne, an American woman who would later become his wife. When the couple married, Fanny was told that her frail, young husband had only months to live. That Stevenson survived for another fourteen years to accomplish his best work was largely due to the devotion, care and self-sacrifice of his wife. Stevenson's major talent lay in his ability to imbue his greatest works, *Treasure Island, Dr. Jekyll and Mr. Hyde,* and *Kidnapped* with both a keen awareness of the supernatural and a lighthearted romanticism, which turned common places and history into poetic, adventurous narrative. By his death in 1894, Stevenson had assured himself a place in English literature and had accomplished far more than his simple desire to "leave an image for a few years upon men's minds."

The Hayloft

*Through all the pleasant meadow-side
The grass grew shoulder-high,
Till the shining scythes went far and wide
And cut it down to dry.*

*These green and sweetly smelling crops
They led in waggons home;
And they piled them here in mountain tops
For mountaineers to roam.*

*Here is Mount Clear, Mount Rusty-Nail,
Mount Eagle and Mount High;
The mice that in these mountains dwell,
No happier are than I!*

*Oh, what a joy to clamber there,
Oh, what a place for play,
With the sweet, the dim, the dusty air,
The happy hills of hay.*

The Vagabond

Give to me the life I love;
Let the lave go by me;
Give the jolly heaven above
And the byway nigh me.
Bed in the bush with stars to see,
Bread I dip in the river—
There's the life for a man like me,
There's the life forever.

Let the blow fall soon or late;
Let what will be o'er me;
Give the face of earth around
And the road before me.
Wealth I seek not, hope nor love,
Nor a friend to know me;
All I seek, the heaven above
And the road below me.

Or let autumn fall on me
Where afield I linger,
Silencing the bird on tree,
Biting the blue finger.
White as meal the frosty field,
Warm the fireside haven—
Not to autumn will I yield,
Not to winter even!

Let the blow fall soon or late,
Let what will be o'er me;
Give the face of earth around,
And the road before me.
Wealth I ask not, hope nor love,
Nor a friend to know me;
All I ask, the heaven above
And the road below me.

The Gardener

The gardener does not love to talk,
He makes me keep the gravel walk;
And when he puts his tools away,
He locks the door and takes the key.

Away behind the currant row
Where no one else but cook may go,
Far in the plots, I see him dig,
Old and serious, brown and big.

He digs the flowers, green, red, and blue,
Nor wishes to be spoken to.
He digs the flowers and cuts the hay,
And never seems to want to play.

Silly gardener! Summer goes,
And winter comes with pinching toes,
When in the garden bare and brown
You must lay your barrow down.

Well now, and while the summer stays,
To profit by these garden days,
Oh, how much wiser you would be
To play at Indian wars with me!

Farewell to the Farm

The coach is at the door at last;
The eager children, mounting fast
And kissing hands, in chorus sing:
Goodbye, goodbye, to everything!

To house and garden, field and lawn,
The meadow gates we swang upon,
To pump and stable, tree and swing,
Goodbye, goodbye, to everything!

And fare you well for evermore,
O ladder at the hayloft door,
O hayloft where the cobwebs cling,
Goodbye, goodbye, to everything!

Crack goes the whip, and off we go;
The trees and houses smaller grow;
Last, round the woody turn we swing:
Goodbye, goodbye, to everything!

The Spirit
☆ of America—1980 ☆

The spirit of America is showing
    As we travel this land coast to coast.
Our people still stand to honor the flag
    That attests to those freedoms we boast.

Old memories shared are part of it all.
    Men of faith fought and died for its birth.
That spirit, like bugle notes played from the heart,
    Is sounding our anthem all over the earth.

Fifty states, individually united,
    Have a strength that withstands every test.
Tempests rage, protests march in their season—
    United we stand for the right and the best.

America is more than possessions.
    Back in history her saga begins.
Strife and struggle add strength to her lessons
    That are based on faith, family and friends.

From each city, village, town, every suburb—
    All over this land far and wide,
The spirit of America is growing,
    Where the people choose God as their guide.
                  Alice Leedy Mason

This beautiful painting by John Slobodnik
is featured on Ideals' special patriotic issue
The Spirit of America. For ordering
information, please turn to the last page.

A Taste of New England

Within the vast borders of the U.S.A. travelers have come to know each particular region by the culinary fare it has to offer. The Midwest is synonymous with tender, juicy beef. The South is justifiably proud of its golden fried chicken. And the Southwest receives rave reviews for its spicy enchiladas. Journey with us now to the eastern coast and savor some of the seafood specialties which highlight the many pleasures New England has to offer.

AVOCADO-CRAB DIP

1 large avocado, peeled, seeded
  and cubed
1 T. lemon juice
1 T. grated onion
1 t. Worcestershire sauce
1 8-oz. pkg. cream cheese, softened
¼ c. sour cream
¼ t. salt
1 7½-oz. can crab meat, drained,
  flaked and cartilage removed

In small bowl combine avocado, lemon juice, onion and Worcestershire sauce. Beat until smooth. Add cream cheese, sour cream, and salt; blend. Add crab; refrigerate. Serve with crackers. Serves 8.

SLIMMER CRAB CAKES

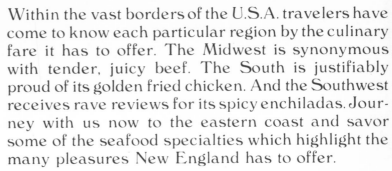

1 t. prepared mustard
2 T. salad dressing
1 egg
1 lb. crab meat
  Salt and pepper
¼ t. dry mustard
½ c. cracker meal
¼ c. chopped parsley
  Vegetable oil

Mix prepared mustard, salad dressing and egg together; add crab meat, seasonings, mustard, cracker meal, and parsley. Mix lightly so as not to break up the crab meat. Form into cakes. Fry in small amount of oil until brown; turn and brown on other side. Cakes may also be broiled. Serves 4.

SEAFOOD CASSEROLE

1 lb. cooked shrimp
4 T. butter
½ c. minced onion
½ c. minced green pepper
1 10½-oz. can cream of mushroom soup
¾ c. milk
1 2-oz. can chopped mushrooms, with
  liquid
3 c. cooked rice
1 6½-oz. can crab meat, drained, flaked,
  and cartilage removed
1 c. buttered bread crumbs
½ c. grated Cheddar cheese

Set aside 10 whole shrimp. Cut remaining shrimp in half and set aside. Melt butter in medium-size saucepan and sauté onion and green pepper until tender. Add soup, milk, and mushrooms with liquid; simmer 10 minutes. Fold in rice. Set aside 1½ cups of mixture. To remaining mixture, add cut shrimp and crab meat. Pour in a 2-quart greased casserole. Top with remaining soup mixture; sprinkle with bread crumbs and cheese. Split remaining shrimp lengthwise and arrange on top of casserole. Bake in a 350° oven for 30 minutes. Serves 8.

LOBSTER NEWBURG

2 c. cubed, cooked lobster
¼ c. butter
½ t. salt
  Dash of cayenne
  Dash of nutmeg
½ c. cream
2 egg yolks, lightly beaten
2 T. sherry

Lightly sauté lobster in butter for 3 minutes. Add seasonings and heat 1 minute. Add cream and egg yolks; simmer 3 minutes more. Add sherry and serve in chafing dish. Serves 2 to 4.

Homossassa Jungle In Florida
by Winslow Homer

Florida

I open eyes to mornings crowned with gold
By a sun I've never seen before,
So close to earth it burns, so bright, so bold.
I hear the song of sea that sprays the shore;
I open windows to its siren cry.
And there it is, a world so wide and blue,
With waves and clouds to show where sea meets sky.
I hear palm branches blow with rustling sound,
Like full, starched skirts
That dance and sweep the ground.
I smell the perfume of a thousand flowers
Of blooming plants and shrubs that I can't name.
They glow in clusters, vines and bowers,
Jewel-like in color and wax-like to feel,
So lovely to behold, too perfect to be real.
I walk on white sand beaches in bare feet
And gather washed-up treasures from the deep;
Curved seashells, coral lace, a crab's retreat—
All these, and memories, for me to keep

Annabel Hemley

Paradise

Words, mere words, cannot suffice
To tell the charms of Paradise!
Sky and sea of heavenly blue,
Gay umbrellas tint the view;
Sand and clouds are snowy white—
Whiter for the sun so bright.
Foamy tides lap on the shore.
'Cross the reef you hear a roar!
Look! The surf is dashing high,
Shawls of lace against the sky!

Soon the wind will die away,
Fading with it, surf and spray;
Then upon those sands is rest—
Nature at her loveliest!
Neath the rustling palms, the sea
Bids you "Come and drowse with me.
Lose yourself and dream away;
There's no morrow, just today."

Fred Winslow Rust

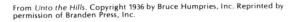

Blue Ridge Legacy

Mountains are beautiful
Stretching so high.
Green, leafy branches
Lace-up the sky.
Breezes float gently
On gossamer wings.
Truly God's mountains
Are heavenly things.

Mountains—those lofty
Breathtaking sights.
Fog cloaks their mornings;
Stars gem their nights.
Layer on layer
They come into view,
Ridges of mountains,
Misty and blue.

Mountains are powerful,
Rugged and vast.
Hill, ridge and hollow are
Things that will last.
Standing knee-deep in
The eons of time . . .
Blessed is the child
With mountains to climb!

Alice Leedy Mason

The Land of Evangeline

This is the forest primeval.
The murmuring pines and the hemlocks,
Bearded with moss,
And in garments green,
Indistinct in the twilight,
Stand like Druids of eld,
With voices sad and prophetic,
Stand like harpers hoar,
With beards that rest on their bosoms.
Loud from its rocky caverns,
The deep-voiced neighboring ocean
Speaks and in accents disconsolate
Answers the wail of the forest.

From Evangeline

This is the forest primeval;
But where are the hearts that beneath it
Leaped like the roe,
When he hears in the woodland
The voice of the huntsman?
Where is the thatch-roofed village,
The home of Acadian farmers—
Men whose lives glided on like rivers
That water the woodlands,
Darkened by shadows of earth,
But reflecting an image of heaven?
Waste are those pleasant farms,
And the farmers forever departed!
Scattered like dust and leaves,
When the mighty blasts of October
Seize them, and whirl them aloft,
And sprinkle them far o'er the ocean.
Naught but tradition remains
Of the beautiful village of Grand-Pré.

Ye who believe in affection
That hopes, and endures, and is patient,
Ye who believe in the beauty
And strength of woman's devotion,
List to the mournful tradition,
Still sung by the pines of the forest;
List to a tale of love in Acadie,
Home of the happy.

Henry Wadsworth Longfellow

The Road That Leads to Home

Of all the roads on land or sea
My feet have chanced to roam,
The loveliest of them to me,
Is the road that leads to home.

The road that leads to home, it seems,
Is dearer than the rest,
For it is paved with fondest dreams
Of those I love the best.

It has a friendliness, a cheer,
This road that brings me back
To home and those I love so dear,
That all the others lack.

It is the one road I can wend,
When weary, worn, and spent
And know that waiting at its end,
I shall find peace, content.

Harry E. Brainard

NO POSTAGE
NECESSARY
IF MAILED
IN THE
UNITED STATES

BUSINESS REPLY CARD
FIRST CLASS   PERMIT NO. 5761   MILWAUKEE, WI

 *ideals*

PUBLISHING CORPORATION
11315 WATERTOWN PLANK RD.
MILWAUKEE, WISCONSIN 53226

NO POSTAGE
NECESSARY
IF MAILED
IN THE
UNITED STATES

BUSINESS REPLY CARD
FIRST CLASS   PERMIT NO. 5761   MILWAUKEE, WI

ideals

PUBLISHING CORPORATION
11315 WATERTOWN PLANK RD.
MILWAUKEE, WISCONSIN 53226

Share

treasured moments with someone you love
in our next issue, Grandparent's *ideals* . . .

- Enjoy a salute to Grandparents in heart-warming prose, poetry, illustrations, and beautiful color photography.

- Feature articles include a journey to Niagara Falls, reminiscences from a fifty-year reunion, and antique trunks as collectors' items.

- Enhance your reading enjoyment or share this delightful keepsake with the special people in your life. A subscription is a thoughtful gift for everyone . . . from children to their parents or grandparents or for a special friend. Fill out either attached card and mail today!

My Old Kentucky Home

Stephen Foster

The sun shines bright on the old Kentucky home,
'Tis summer, the darkies are gay.
The corn-top's ripe and the meadow's in the bloom,
While the birds make music all the day.
The young folks roll on the little cabin floor,
All merry, all happy, and bright.
By 'n' by hard times come a-knocking at the door,
Then, my old Kentucky home, good night!

They hunt no more for the 'possum and the 'coon
On the meadow, the hill, and the shore.
They sing no more by the glimmer of the moon,
On the bench by the old cabin door.
The day goes by like a shadow o'er the heart,
With sorrow where all was delight.
The time has come when the darkies have to part,
Then, my old Kentucky home, good night!

The head must bow and the back will have to bend
Wherever the darky may go.
A few more days and the trouble all will end,
In the fields where the sugarcanes grow,
A few more days for to tote the weary load,
No matter, 'twill never be light,
A few more days till we totter on the road,
Then, my old Kentucky home, good night!

Chorus
Weep no more, my lady,
Oh, weep no more today!
We will sing one song for the old Kentucky home,
For the old Kentucky home, far away.

The beauty and spirit of the Old South are nowhere better recorded than in the lyrics of Stephen Foster, the greatest American composer of the nineteenth century. Best loved are his nostalgic songs and plantation melodies describing life in the Antebellum South. Born in Pennsylvania, Foster never visited the South until he married, yet, his earliest songs reflected a real knowledge of Southern living. Growing up along the Ohio River, young Foster was exposed to the songs and tales of the South by the river traffic to and from New Orleans. He fell in love with the music at a Negro church which he visited with the family's West Indian servant. A strong love for home and family came to be an integral part of his music. His most famous song, "Old Folks at Home," better known as "Way Down upon the Swanee River," was written in 1851. A visit to the Bardstown, Kentucky, home of a relative inspired the writing of his next famous song in 1853. "My Old Kentucky Home," written in the traditional Foster style, created a new era in American folk music. It was adopted as the state song of Kentucky in 1928. The music of America's greatest composer of folk songs, Stephen Foster, was never fully appreciated until years after his death.

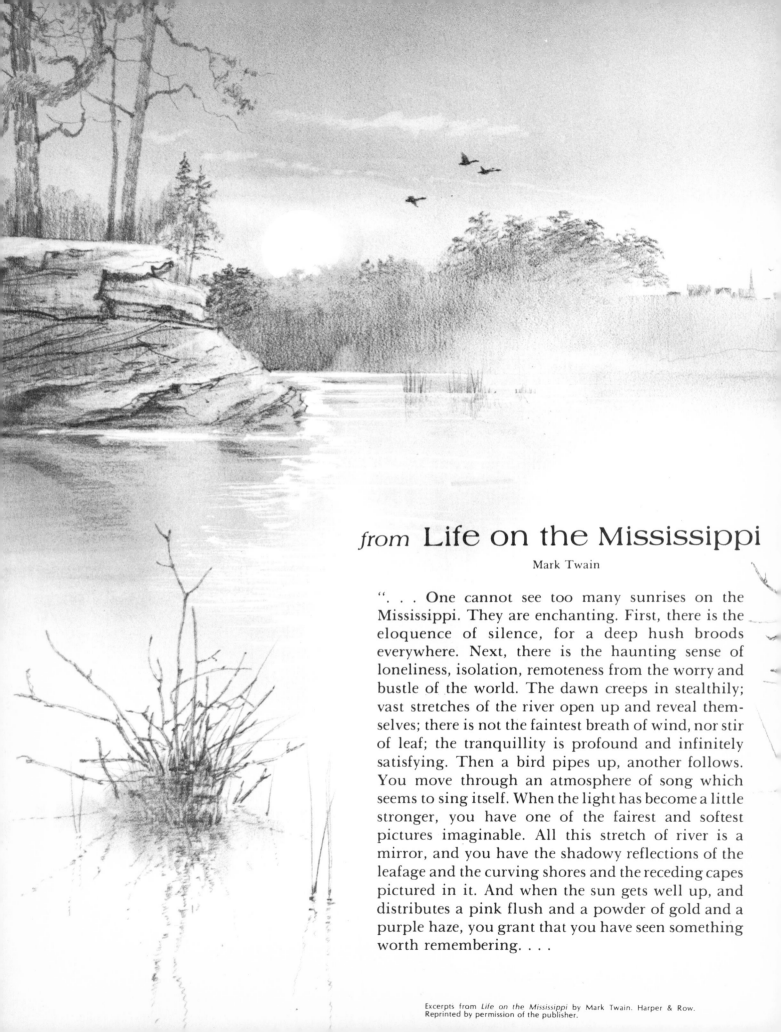

from Life on the Mississippi

Mark Twain

". . . One cannot see too many sunrises on the Mississippi. They are enchanting. First, there is the eloquence of silence, for a deep hush broods everywhere. Next, there is the haunting sense of loneliness, isolation, remoteness from the worry and bustle of the world. The dawn creeps in stealthily; vast stretches of the river open up and reveal themselves; there is not the faintest breath of wind, nor stir of leaf; the tranquillity is profound and infinitely satisfying. Then a bird pipes up, another follows. You move through an atmosphere of song which seems to sing itself. When the light has become a little stronger, you have one of the fairest and softest pictures imaginable. All this stretch of river is a mirror, and you have the shadowy reflections of the leafage and the curving shores and the receding capes pictured in it. And when the sun gets well up, and distributes a pink flush and a powder of gold and a purple haze, you grant that you have seen something worth remembering. . . .

Excerpts from *Life on the Mississippi* by Mark Twain. Harper & Row.
Reprinted by permission of the publisher.

". . . The majestic bluffs that overlook the river, along through this region, charm one with the grace and variety of their forms, and the soft beauty of their adornment. The steep, verdant slope, whose base is at the water's edge, is topped by a lofty rampart of broken, turreted rocks, which are exquisitely rich and mellow in color—mainly dark browns and dull greens, but splashed with other tints. And then you have the shining river, winding here and there and yonder, its sweep interrupted at intervals by clusters of wooded islands threaded by silver channels; and you have glimpses of distant villages, asleep upon capes, and of stealthy rafts slipping along in the shade of the forest walls, and of white steamers vanishing around remote points. And it is all as tranquil and reposeful as dreamland, and has nothing this-worldly about it—nothing to hang a fret or a worry upon. . ."

Secrets in Sandstone

The backwater in the gorge is calm, unlike the swift flow of the Wisconsin River's main channel only a few yards beyond the cliff face. But in here, in the dim quiet of the canyon, the tannin colored water forms a still, black pool, broken only by the rolling backs of several huge carp. A tiny stab of sunlight pierces the overhead mantle of ferns and pines atop the cliffs, spotlighting the fish in a rainbow explosion off their shining, wet scales.

Rain coursing down the sides of the sandstone walls has scoured deep grooves along the face of the living stone, as if a playful, giant cat had sharpened its claws after missing a swipe at the fat, lazy fish.

Shadows in the gulch are as deep as the pool, hinting at long-forgotten answers to secrets known only to the cliffs. Cool and dark, even on the hottest summer days, the canyon seems untouched, undisturbed, impervious to the passage of travelers who have explored its recesses for the past hundred years. The rocks, water, damp moss, fish—all ignore that passing and continue on as they have for eons.

The river rolls hungrily along outside, on its 420-mile meandering journey across the face of Wisconsin, from the northern borders with Michigan to its muddy junction with the Mississippi River in the southwestern part of the state. Here in the heart of Wisconsin, the river breaks from the flatlands to twist and turn as would a captured king snake. Five hundred million years ago, the prehistoric seas crashed across this landscape three times, say the geologists, to lay down the thick layers of stone.

Then came the river, long after the oceans had receded. Over the generations—allied with the wind, rain and rock-shattering frost—that water continued its work of wearing away the sandstone, pausing to carve intricate designs in what are now soaring cliffs. For seven and one-fifth miles, the river moves past and through this ageless handiwork.

The resulting formations make up what are known today as the Wisconsin Dells, tourist attractions since the first Indian hunters seven thousand years ago reported their find to neighboring friends. Woodland tribes settled in, creating delicate pottery with designs taken from nature's own. Then, five thousand years ago, came the Mound Builders; though awed by the enormity of the cliffs, they fashioned and molded the land for their own sacred uses.

More tribes followed over the ensuing years: Winnebagoes, Sauk and Chippewas were only the latest in a succession of peoples who appreciated and loved the area they called *Nee-ah-ke-coonah-er-ah*, or "the place where the rocks strike together or nearly strike together."

Even now it is easy to recall the Indian legends about how the land was formed. Imagine the Great Spirit in the form of a huge snake smashing his way southward from his frozen lakeside home in the north's dense forests. The river swiftly fills the channel dug by the crawling body. The Great Spirit arrives at the rock ridges, part of a spiny range extending toward the Mississippi. He shoves his head through one crevice, then bursts through. His approach frightens off the lesser deities, who are also disguised as snakes.

They flee, their escape routes becoming the canyons leading off from the main chasm. Such is the stuff of dreams.

French-Canadian voyagers in their long, fur-filled freight canoes came hard on the heels of the tribesmen. They used their word *dalles*, meaning trough or narrow passage, to describe this section of the Wisconsin River. From the subsequent slurring of the word and accent change evolved the word *Dells*.

The Dells truly caught the traveler's fancy shortly after the Civil War when former lumberman and river pilot Leroy Gates announced that he had purchased a pleasure boat. Gates said the vessel could be used for exploring the "numerous occult caves of the district." His pitch went on to promise that "depressed spirits can be alleviated, gloom and melancholy soon dispelled and the mind greatly invigorated" by a riverboat tour.

At the same time, stereoscopic slides of the Dells taken by noted photographer H.H. Bennett became more popular. As the fame of these natural wonders spread across the country, tourists began flocking to central Wisconsin.

Ever since, the Dells have been among the most popular attractions in the Midwest. While commercial developments have sprung up in the small communities near the river, the Wisconsin remains all-powerful—still carving, chipping and creating.

The Upper Dells, north of a huge dam in the city of Wisconsin Dells, are home for numerous fanciful formations named over the years by passersby: Swallow's Nest, High Rock, Romance Cliff, Black Hawk's Head, Giant's Shield, Alligator's Head and others. Almost every outcropping has a tag. Cold Water Canyon, Witches' Gulch and Stand Rock lead off from the main river and are showcases for the tour guides. On the Lower Dells, below the dam, are the Witches' Window, the Football, Grand Piano, the Rocky Islands, Ink Stand and similar geographic delights—their names indicating their shapes.

The seasons bring lovely, everchanging intricacies to the Dells. Spring urges the delicate wild flowers to carpet the clifftops. Summer paints a heavy olivine across the land, with only the white birches in bas-relief. Autumn dances across the woods, making the world shimmer in a thousand hues. Winter's harshness hardens the river's surface, but never its vibrant soul.

The Dells are constant and steady, always delightful. In the soft ever-evening shadows of the canyons, while the fish play tag with the sun streams, the secrets of this land may be revealed. But the visitor must listen, watch and, most importantly, dream a bit.

Martin Hintz

"Back Roads" Beauty

Bea Bourgeois

One of our national tendencies seems to be an obsession with speed. Particularly when we travel by car, "What time did you leave?" becomes a question of the utmost importance. It is almost a point of honor to shave fifteen or twenty minutes off the established driving time between, for example, Milwaukee and northern Wisconsin.

Freeways—those monotonous, hypnotic stretches of pale concrete—have one advantage: they take the traveler from Point A to Point B in the shortest possible amount of time. But we've discovered that speed isn't everything.

A few years ago we invested in a set of County Maps of Wisconsin, available from the Department of Transportation for $3.50 plus tax. The 72 maps are alphabetically arranged, so it's easy to plot a trip up and down or across the state. My husband put the maps in a sturdy three-ring binder, and we keep the book under the front seat of the car.

That book has become a magical "Open Sesame" for our family. We have abandoned the popular I-94 route for our trips to Hayward, and instead we use Wisconsin's state and county roads. We may not break any speed records, but we've discovered some wonderful things about Wisconsin and the people who live here.

Of course, we have been occasionally stuck behind a tractor or a milk truck for a few miles, but so what? We've had a chance to see endless acres of sunflowers being raised for seed; huge fields of potatoes near Stevens Point; a beautiful stray deer poised hesitantly at the edge of a woods; mink and turkey farms, some with spooky, old, abandoned buildings; real, working farmers plowing and threshing their land—rare sights for city dwellers.

When we left Milwaukee at Eastertime one year, we drove as far as Princeton, in Green Lake County, and stopped for breakfast. Purely by chance we discovered a bright and cheery "Ma and Pa" cafe where several local residents were trading jokes over their morning coffee.

Our meal was scrumptious: freshly fried eggs, hot buttered toast, crisp pork sausage, and French toast sizzling from the griddle. Coffee cups were refilled regularly, always with a smile and a friendly remark. It was a pleasure to eat food that had not been precooked and prepackaged.

About an hour out of Princeton our youngest son discovered that he had left a favorite cap in the restaurant. On the way back to Milwaukee, after nearly a week had passed, we stopped at the cafe and were stunned when the smiling, grandmotherly cook handed David his cap. "I saved it for you," she explained with a grin. I'm not sure, but somehow I don't think that would have happened at an ultra modern, fast-food franchise restaurant!

We passed through thirteen different Wisconsin counties on that trip. In tiny towns, we stopped at grocery stores for treats of all kinds; we bought fresh eggs along the way; we marveled at the sea of red cranberries in storage tanks near Wisconsin Rapids, where the road cuts right between the bogs.

We stretched our legs in small rural cemeteries and were awed by the antiquity of some of the grave markers. We were able to show our sons what wild asparagus looks like, and we stopped at a farm to buy a bag of straw that made a comfortable bed for the Infant in the Christmas creche months later.

After driving through paper mill country near Nekoosa and Port Edwards, we went west on highway 73 into Clark County where we discovered a lovely County Park outside of Greenwood. We had packed a picnic lunch and were blessed with a sunny, mild day; it was a refreshing pause to munch our sandwiches in the park with a gentle, flowing river for a backdrop. The boys worked off some excess energy throwing sticks into the river and Frisbees at one another.

We have happened onto county fairs and small town anniversary celebrations, and been overwhelmed with local hospitality. We have meandered through intriguing antique shops in out-of-the-way places. We have enjoyed some of Wisconsin's lovely spring wildflowers—marsh marigolds, violets, trilliums, buttercups, and Indian paint brushes.

Farm youngsters have waved to the toot of our horn from their perches high on a tractor or a hay wagon. Their parents have shared a luscious raspberry harvest with us—for significantly less than we would have paid at the supermarket. Old advertising signs on barns and fence posts have brought back memories of gentler times when speed didn't matter at all.

Traveling the state and county highways has given us an unbeatable opportunity to learn more about Wisconsin and to appreciate its people. Our family is convinced that superhighways are efficient, fast, and boring. We don't mind a raised eyebrow or two when we answer the inevitable "How long did it take you?" There are a lot of advantages to being slow pokes!

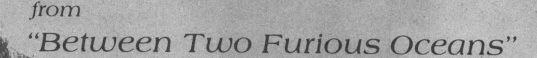

from
"Between Two Furious Oceans"

You are the quiet bays and the lonely shadows of the firs;
The vast green acres blanketing the wide Alberni hills,
    Hemlock and cedar and spruce . . . proud with everlasting green;
    Cold blue glaciers, spilling their life into roaring Atlin creeks;

Meadows in the clouds and valleys mute with solitude . . .
    You are the heaving lakes, the rolling, green-jacketed hills
    Of Stormont and Dundas; roaring Niagara and the swift
    Cold current of the Ottawa, hedged with silver birch . . .

You are the dainty meadows and the lazy, dappled streams
Of Joliette; the cool, sweet whisper of Laurentian breezes;
    The river willows and the gracious elms; chipmunk and beaver
    And the antlered deer; the green, windswept curve of Gaspé loin . . .

You are the caravans that spanned the plains and the axe that hewed
The cedars for Camosun's Fort; you are the arm that fought
    The torrent through Kicking Horse, paddling to the ocean from the heights . . .

You are a new nation, the raw nugget;
    The untempered blade, the uncontrolled flame . . .
    You are the white-hot steel, taking your shape
    Under the hammerblows of Time. . . .

Dick Diespecker

In a little while all interest was taken up in stretching our necks and watching for the pony-rider—the fleet messenger who sped across the continent from St. Joe to Sacramento, carrying letters nineteen hundred miles in eight days!

The Pony Express
Samuel Clemens

R. Adams

Think of that for perishable horse and human flesh and blood to do! The pony-rider was usually a little bit of a man, brimful of spirit and endurance. No matter what time of the day or night his watch came on, and no matter whether it was winter or summer, raining, snowing, hailing, or sleeting, or whether his beat was a level, straight road or a crazy trail over mountain crags and precipices, or whether it led through peaceful regions or regions that swarmed with hostile Indians, he must be always ready to leap into the saddle and be off like the wind! There was no idling-time for a pony-rider on duty. He rode fifty miles without stopping, by daylight, moonlight, starlight, or through the blackness of darkness—just as it happened. He rode a splendid horse that was born for a racer and fed and lodged like a gentleman, kept him at his utmost speed for ten miles, and then, as he came crashing up to the station where stood two men holding fast a fresh, impatient steed, the transfer of rider and mailbag was made in the twinkling of an eye, and away flew the eager pair and were out of sight

Today, the Badlands are more easily accessible via reinforced trails and a paved road. At the heart of the monument, Cedar Pass provides a museum, campground and visitor center, which offers daytime nature hikes and nighttime amphitheater programs. Without disturbing the natural environment, these conveniences keep within reach the wild and transient beauty of the Badlands.

Several miles to the west, however, a more permanent landmark, this one man-made, promises to endure through the ages both physically and spiritually.

Over half a century ago, the peaceful serenity of the Black Hills was shattered by drilling jackhammers and exploding dynamite. Sculptor Gutzon Borglum had begun his most difficult yet intriguing challenge: to carve on the exposed face of a towering granite bluff America's shrine to democracy—Mount Rushmore National Memorial. Fourteen years later, and with no finer tools than these ordinarily destructive forces, Borglum had created a masterpiece of artistry and engineering dedicated to the principles, dreams and aspirations of an entire nation.

Originally conceived by state historian Doane Robinson as a tribute to the heroic figures of the west, the project took on a more significant dimension when he approached well-known artist, Gutzon Borglum with his plan. The idealistic artist believed that the mountain should stand not only for the west, but for the whole country as well. He was convinced that no one could better personify those qualities responsible for America's perpetuation than the Presidents of the United States. For that reason, and for their outstanding examples of leadership, Borglum selected George Washington, Thomas Jefferson, Theodore Roosevelt and Abraham Lincoln for his mountain monument.

In 1927, Borglum and his trained crew dangled over the edge of the 6,000-foot cliff in bosuns' chairs, and began chipping away at the granite wall. From small-scale plaster models they fashioned granite heads sixty feet in height. Although they intended to carve the figures complete to the waist, the heads alone eventually required nearly fourteen years to finish.

They encountered many delays caused by the rock's stubbornness. The biggest setback occurred when it became obvious that the granite would not conform to the contours of the first face. Forced to abandon this first attempt, Borglum had to blast it off the mountain. But these delays were never a waste of time, only valuable learning experiences essential in preventing future delays.

Finally, after battling through almost half a million tons of tough, unyielding rock, the aging artist/engineer saw his sculpture nearing completion. In 1941, at the age of seventy-four, Gutzon Borglum died, leaving a lasting tribute to America in the land of *Paha-Sapa*.

The Black Hills are still the sacred land of the spirits, especially the spirit of America.

Rachel Knight

There's a church in the valley by the wildwood,
No lovelier spot in the dale;
No place is so dear to my childhood
As the little brown church in the vale.

Oh, come to the church in the wildwood,
To the trees where the wild flowers bloom;
Where the parting hymn will be chanted,
We will weep by the side of the tomb.

From the church in the valley by the wildwood,
When day fades away into night,
I would fain from this spot of my childhood
Wing my way to the mansions of light.

Oh, come, come, come, come,
Come to the church in the wildwood;
Oh, come to the church in the vale;
No spot is so dear to my childhood
As the little brown church in the vale.

William S. Pitts

The Little Brown Church in the Vale

On many a Sunday morning in church, people have sung the uplifting words, "Come to the church in the wildwood; come to the church in the vale." The romantic birth of this song, "The Church in the Wildwood," is linked to another equally inspiring story—that of the coincidental building of an actual church which came to be known as "The Little Brown Church in the Vale."

The story began in 1857, when a young music teacher, William S. Pitts, traveling by stagecoach from his home in southern Wisconsin to visit his bride-to-be in Fredericksburg, Iowa, stopped for a rest at noon in the little pioneer town of Bradford, Iowa. As the young, enamored Pitts strolled through town, he came to a spot of rare and tranquil beauty. He was deeply touched by the loveliness and serenity of the scene, and visualized a small, rural church set amidst the rolling green hills, lush foliage and ancient trees. When Pitts returned home, his thoughts drifted back to the image of a country church in the midst of that pastoral setting. The young music teacher sat down and wrote the song, "The Little Brown Church in the Vale," then put the composition away in a desk drawer where it remained gathering dust.

When Pitts returned to Bradford years later, he was stunned by what he saw. In the six years that had passed, the people of Bradford had decided to build a church right in the very spot where Pitts had imagined one. The project was begun in 1859 when Rev. John K. Nutting came to Bradford to serve as pastor. At that time, the people were worshipping in a log cabin, a lawyer's office, a hotel dining room, a school house and an abandoned store without doors or windows. The members of the church were few in number and poor, but they were inspired by the young pastor to try to build a church. The struggling congregation of pioneers contributed most of the logs, lumber, and stones and much of the work to finish the building. The bell in the tower was donated by a couple in New York, and its coming was such a wondrous event that it was rung constantly during its trip from Dubuque to Bradford.

On dedication day in 1864, Mr. Pitts' voice class sang his song about the "little brown church" in public for the first time. Soon afterwards, Pitts took the song to Chicago, where it was published. He used the money he earned from its publication to help finance his schooling for a medical degree, then returned with his wife to Fredericksburg, where he set up practice. The song quickly won local recognition, but little did its author know that one day it would capture the hearts and minds of people across the land and around the world.

At the turn of the century, the church became inactive for a time when the community of Bradford all but disappeared after the town failed to acquire a railroad. However, a railroad did come to the nearby town of Nashua, which steadily grew as the town of Bradford declined. For a time, the church building was closed, and weeds grew high across the unkept grounds. Its brown paint soon lost its luster, but the stouthearted little congregation kept faith in someday witnessing the church's revival. They could never have foreseen the future fame of their little "church in the vale."

In 1910, a group of vocalists from Iowa known as the "Weatherwax Brothers Male Quartet," who were gaining in popularity, performing at chautauquas and social gatherings around the country and Canada, introduced the song into their programs. With each singing they would tell the story of how Dr. Pitts wrote the song and the location of the real church in the wildwood. Out of a repertoire of more than three hundred numbers, "The Church in the Wildwood," as it was later renamed, was the one song America remembered.

Today, situated in the little northeast Iowa town of Nashua, the church continues to grow. Many thousands of visitors each year have journeyed to "the little brown church." Some have come for the sacrament of baptism, some to take vows of matrimony, and others, simply to experience the same peace, comfort and joy that a young music teacher felt and recorded in a prophetic song more than a hundred years ago.

Michele Arrieh

Arizona

Come with me to Arizona,
a copper land of flowing mountains
brown with age,
rainbow gorges, desert sand and purple sage
where a thousand miles of sunset throw
a fading glow
into a star-filled night.

Then when morning rises, take my hand
and linger
in this golden land with me
where barefoot boys and barefoot girls
stayed and built adobe dreams.

Listen!
Happy laughter fills the spaces.
Sturdy cacti
bare their faces to the blistering sun.
Farther on,
away from dust, lie emerald valleys.

Follow me
and I will show you hidden trails,
mountain pastures,
crystal water cold as ice
with fish,
and air with spice of cedar tree and pine
where deer and squirrel live
in primal paradise.

Almyra Noller

Four Corners: Gateway to the Southwest

Beverly Wiersum Charette

Travelers following U.S. 160 spot the sign indicating "Point of interest ahead" and pull off the highway. Forcing themselves out of their air-conditioned, 72-degree cars into the sun-conditioned, 100-degree desert, they glance around expectantly, hoping to marvel at another of nature's remarkably artistic accomplishments peculiar to this area. Instead, they are greeted by a lonely, man-made marker set in stone labeled "Four Corners"—the only point in the United States common to four states. In the midst of a remote and desolate desert, the cornerstone of America's southwest struggles to remain above the sand.

Initially, this point of interest, shared by Colorado, New Mexico, Arizona and Utah, leaves visitors with an impression far from interesting; in all four directions the eyes meet nothing but sun, sand and sagebrush. The marker itself seems ludicrous, relying on imaginary man-made boundaries as a meaning for existence. But upon more thoughtful inspection, the seasoned traveler, no stranger to the artistry of erosion commonplace in this part of the country, appreciates the marker's simplicity as it stands sentinel over the unique scenic beauty typical of the southwest.

Slender arches of burnt ocher defy gravity, spanning incredible distances with no other support than the air. Large, odd-shaped boulders balance precariously on pinpoint supports, threatening to topple at any moment. Others cling stubbornly to a smooth, sloping rock surface like crumbs to a cookie sheet. The mouth of a stone monkey's head is frozen in mid-chatter. In this delusory state of suspended animation the only movement is the subtle stirring of the wind—the heartbeat of the southwest—lightly fingering the sandstone formations of Arches National Park.

In reality, these stone sculptures are undergoing a continuous process of decay caused by nature's eroding forces. This greatest concentration of natural arches in the world began forming long ago when the earth bulged out of its seams and cracked an entire layer of sandstone. Rain, frost and thaw, and other weathering agents widened these cracks until they cut through a narrow wall, or "fin," to form a hole. Subsequent rockfalls enlarged the hole, creating an arch. Eventually all the graceful arches of the southwest, including the eighty-eight discovered within the boundaries of this park, will collapse, leaving only their end buttresses to jut out into the desert sun.

But the arches have many years left before crumbling into oblivion. Visitors can still experience nature's artistry in the land of eternal sunset.

An overly ambitious maid, the mighty southwestern wind sweeps up from the direction of Four Corners and attacks the unanchored silt and sand of the San Luis Valley in south central Colorado. Vacuuming up this debris, dragged down from the mountains by rivers and streams, the wind carries it across the flat, open plain to the foot of the Sangre de Cristo range. Here, the nearly impenetrable horseshoe barrier formed by the mountains forces the wind to surrender its heavy burden before whistling through the gaps and openings in the range. Raining sand, the wind shapes a miniature western Sahara—Great Sand Dunes National Monument.

These mountainous dunes represent centuries of the slow yet constant eastward progression of sand in the San Luis River Valley. The sand dunes originate by accumulating around some object, usually a rare sample of hardy plant life. As the wind continues to deposit sand, shifting it from windward to leeward, the dunes begin to advance toward the mountains. En route, they engulf anything that crosses their path, often leaving skeletons of trees in their wake.

Though dwarfed by the nearby mountains, including some of the highest peaks in the continental divide, the Great Sand Dunes are the tallest dunes in the United States, some towering over 700 feet. Against the shadowy, jagged peaks of the southern Rockies, the dunes stand out in brilliant, smooth contrast.

As the Guadalupe Mountains consume the liquid, desert sun, an intense stillness pervades the atmosphere, overwhelming the uninvited intruders. Then, barely perceptible, the silence of moving air emanates from the depths of the yawning hole opposite the audience. Building to a crescendo, this silence explodes into a flutter of swirling wings; the night sky over Carlsbad Caverns National Park, New Mexico, is alive with the 300,000 residents of Bat Cave.

Unquestionably a remarkable spectacle, this nightly exodus was what originally lured the first white men to investigate the deceivingly empty land along New Mexico's southern border. Searching for the point of origin of this great black horde's nocturnal raid on insects, they discovered not only Bat Cave, but also the ground-level entrance cave leading to an enormous subterranean system of corridors and chambers. More than 800 feet directly beneath the desert floor, the interior of nature's netherworld palace lay hidden.

Today, visitors can reach the caverns either by braving a steep, switchback trail, or riding a high-speed elevator. Once inside the fourteen-acre Big Room, the main cavern with a ceiling soaring to 285 feet, they are free to explore the seven miles of caverns open to them. Subtle illumination reveals still, green pools and inverted stone icicles, more accurately referred to as stalagmites, as well as their counterparts, stalactites. In the constant 56-degree dampness, winter or summer, visitors can view these stone sculptures deposited by the slow, interminable seepage of water begun thousands of years ago and continuing today.

Jagged shafts of brilliant white light pierce billowing, black clouds. Enraged by such treatment, the clouds rumble a protest amplified by the depths of a massive chasm. Then, dragging the unsheltered earth into this meteorological battle, they pound the dusty soil with steely torrents. Just when the storm threatens to continue indefinitely, however, the sky steps in as moderator and splits the clouds, emitting radiant sunshine to bathe the stratified canyon walls with a soft, buttery glow. It is small wonder that out of such an event, American composer Ferde Grofé created his *Grand Canyon Suite*.

Often referred to as the eighth wonder of the world, northern Arizona's Grand Canyon of the Colorado has, with good reason, stimulated much creative expression. In beauty and magnitude it cannot be equaled. As a living record of time it stands alone. Written upon its walls are the history and prehistory of the southwest, dating back two billion years. The Colorado River, a meticulous archeologist, persistently excavates the canyon, revealing past seabeds, estuaries, sand dunes, deserts and river deltas, which contain the story of life on earth. That story continues today as new varieties of common plant and animal species, such as the pink Grand Canyon rattlesnake, evolve by adapting to the unique conditions of canyon life.

Whether standing on the mile-deep canyon floor or teetering on the edge of the North Rim, no visitor can escape the immediate and overwhelming power of the Grand Canyon.

Temples of the Lord

How thrilled, we stand beneath the peaks
   That tower up to God
And gaze upon their ragged cliffs,
   Where man has never trod!

Majestic mountains, lofty, bold,
   Projecting in the sky,
Seem mighty temples of the Lord,
   With spires of crags on high.

And all His creatures of the woods,
   The birds that chirp and sing,
The roaming deer, the lizards small,
   Each day are worshiping.

And we, who wander in their midst,
   And up the steep trails climb,
Are moved to cherish only thoughts
   Which are the most sublime.

The wilds of nature kindle strong,
   In most of us, the best.
Their tranquil silence brings a peace,
   Their changing shadows, rest.

And like the psalmist, we look up
   Unto the hills for strength;
Unto the heights, whence cometh help
   For all our needs, at length.

Agnes Davenport Bond

The Eagle

James Gates Percival

Bird of the broad and sweeping wing,
   Thy home is high in heaven,
Where the wide storms their banners fling,
   And the tempest-clouds are driven.
Thy throne is on the mountaintop;
   Thy fields, the boundless air;
And hoary peaks, that proudly prop
   The skies, thy dwellings are.

Thou art perched aloft, on the beetling crag,
   And the waves are white below,
And on, with a haste that cannot lag,
   They rush in an endless flow.
Again thou hast plumed thy wing for flight,
   To lands beyond the sea,
And away, like a spirit wreathed in light,
   Thou hurriest, wild and free.

Lord of the boundless realm of air
   In thy imperial name
The hearts of the bold and ardent dare
   The dangerous path of fame.
Beneath the shade of thy golden wings
   The Roman legions bore,
From the river of Egypt's cloudy springs,
   Their pride to the polar shore.

For thee they fought, for thee they fell,
   And their oath on thee was laid;
To thee the clarions raised their swell,
   And the dying warrior prayed.
Thou wert, through an age of death and fears,
   The image of pride and power,
Till the gathered rage of a thousand years
   Burst forth in one awful hour.

And then, a deluge of wrath it came,
   And the nations shook with dread;
And it swept the earth, till its fields were flame,
   And piled with the mingled dead.
Kings were rolled in the wasteful flood,
   With the low and crouching slave;
And together lay in a shroud of blood,
   The coward and the brave.

And where was then thy fearless flight?
   O'er the dark and mysterious sea,
To the land that caught the setting light,
   The cradle of liberty.

There, on the silent and lonely shore,
   For ages I watched alone,
And the world, in its darkness, asked no more
   Where the glorious bird had flown.

But then, came a bold and hardy few,
   And they breasted the unknown wave;
I saw from far the wandering crew,
   And I knew they were high and brave.
I wheeled around the welcome bark,
   As it sought the desolate shore,
And up to heaven, like a joyous lark,
   My quivering pinions bore.

And now, that bold and hardy few
   Are a nation wide and strong;
And danger and doubt I have led them through
   And they worship me in song;
And over their bright and glancing arms,
   On field, and lake, and sea,
With an eye that fires, and a spell that charms
   I guide them to victory!

before the spectator could get hardly the ghost of a look. Both rider and horse went flying light. The rider's dress was thin, and fitted close; he wore a roundabout, and a skullcap, and tucked his pantaloons into his boot tops like a race-rider. He carried no arms—he carried nothing that was not absolutely necessary, for even the postage of his literary freight was worth five dollars a letter. He got but little frivolous correspondence to carry—his bag had business letters in it, mostly. His horse was stripped of all unnecessary weight, too. He wore a little wafer of a racing-saddle, and no visible blanket. He wore light shoes, or none at all. The little flat mail pockets strapped under the rider's thighs would each hold about the bulk of a child's primer. They held many and many an important business chapter and newspaper letter, but these were written on paper as airy and thin as gold-leaf, nearly, and thus bulk and weight were economized. The stagecoach traveled about a hundred to a hundred and twenty-five miles a day (twenty-four hours), the pony-rider about two hundred and fifty. There were about eighty pony-riders in the saddle all the time, night and day, stretching in a long, scattering procession from Missouri to California, forty flying eastward, and forty toward the west, and among them making four hundred gallant horses earn a stirring livelihood and see a deal of scenery every single day.

We had a consuming desire, from the beginning, to see a pony-rider, but somehow or other all that passed us and all that met us managed to streak by in the night, and so we heard only a whiz and a hail, and the swift phantom of the desert was gone before we could get our heads out of the windows. But now we were expecting one along every moment and would see him in broad daylight. Presently the driver exclaims:

"Here he comes!"

Every neck is stretched further, and every eye strained wider. Away across the endless dead level of the prairie a black speck appears against the sky, and it is plain that it moves. Well, I should think so! In a second or two it becomes a horse and rider, rising and falling, rising and falling—sweeping toward us nearer and nearer—growing more and more distinct, more and more sharply defined—nearer and still nearer, and the flutter of the hoofs comes faintly to the ear—another instant a whoop and a hurrah from our upper deck, a wave of the rider's hand, but no reply, and man and horse burst past our excited faces, and go swinging away like a belated fragment of a storm!

So sudden is it all, and so like a flash of unreal fancy, that but for the flake of white foam left quivering and perishing on a mail-sack after the vision had flashed by and disappeared, we might have doubted whether we had seen any actual horse and man at all, maybe.

We rattled through Scott's Bluffs Pass, by and by. It was along here somewhere that we first came across genuine and unmistakable alkali water in the road, and we cordially hailed it as a first-class curiosity, and a thing to be mentioned with éclat in letters to the ignorant at home. This water gave the road a soapy appearance, and in many places the ground looked as if it had been whitewashed. I think the strange alkali water excited us as much as any wonder we had come upon yet, and I know we felt very complacent and conceited, and better satisfied with life after we had added it to our list of things which we had seen and some other people had not.

We crossed the sandhills near the scene of the Indian mail robbery and massacre of 1856, wherein the driver and conductor perished, and also all the passengers but one, it was supposed; but this must have been a mistake, for at different times afterward on the Pacific coast I was personally acquainted with a hundred and thirty-three or four people who were wounded during that massacre, and barely escaped with their lives. There was no doubt of the truth of it—I had it from their own lips. One of these parties told me that he kept coming across arrowheads in his system for nearly seven years after the massacre; and another of them told me that he was stuck so literally full of arrows that after the Indians were gone and he could raise up and examine himself, he could not restrain his tears, for his clothes were completely ruined.

The most trustworthy tradition avers, however, that only one man, a person named Babbitt, survived the massacre, and he was desperately wounded. He dragged himself on his hands and knee (for one leg was broken) to a station several miles away. He did it during portions of two nights, lying concealed one day and part of another, and for more than forty hours suffering unimaginable anguish from hunger, thirst, and bodily pain. The Indians robbed the coach of everything it contained, including quite an amount of treasure.

Paha-Sapa:
Sacred Land of the Spirits

To the goldseekers they were giant treasure troves in which lay hidden the keys to men's fortunes. To weary pioneers traveling west they were a forest oasis, a relief from the bleached, barren wasteland of *mako sica*—the bad land. To the ten tribes of the Sioux nation they were the center of the world, the sacred land of the spirits, the place to commune with *Wakan Tanka*—the Great Spirit. The Indians called them *Paha-Sapa*—the Black Hills.

Certainly "Black Hills" is no misnomer; from a distance they do appear black, rising out of the flat, colorless grasslands of South Dakota. But at closer range the deep green of ponderosa pine forest, spreading across 5,000 square miles, stands out against the clear, blue sky of the plains. Unlike the adolescent Rockies, these ancient mountains do not severely affect the weather patterns and, therefore, do not experience the inevitable daily drenchings common in the higher ranges. Fair weather and blue skies generally prevail, providing a comfortable atmosphere in which visitors can explore the many swiftly-flowing streams, glassy-surfaced lakes and natural as well as man-made landmarks scattered throughout this region.

Only an hour's drive east of the Black Hills the lunar-like landscape of Badlands National Monument thrusts its sawtooth peaks above the surrounding prairie. Any trip to the Black Hills would be incomplete without a visit to this landmark. In Rapid City, the eastern gateway to the Hills, the

School of Mines displays an exhibit of extinct animals that once roamed the lush swamps of the presently arid Badlands. These animals include not only the camels, saber-toothed cats, fox-sized horses and pig-shaped oreodonts of geologically recent time, but also the alligators, snail-like ammonites and giant sea turtles of prehistory.

As these fossilized life forms testify, the Badlands originated as the floor of a shallow inland sea. After the same forces that elevated the Rocky Mountains lifted and drained this floor, small streams cut rolling hills and broad valleys. Raging rivers later stormed down from the mountains with much rocky debris, leveling the former sea bottom into a vast floodplain. As the subsequent marshes evaporated into the present grasslands, nature's eroding forces carved out of this mountain sediment the fantastic shapes of the Badlands.

Such forces continue to strip away these deceptive mountains, laying bare the source of their descriptive and highly appropriate name. Although they have the appearance of solid rock, the mud- and siltstone Badlands do not have the substance of rock to combat the rains and melting snows constantly and rapidly dissolving their fragile crust. Underneath this dry, protective crust, the soil is sodden, slippery and, as a result, very difficult to traverse. Without the modern-day convenience of established paths, the early trailblazers—Indians and French Canadian trappers—found the terrain nearly impossible to cross; hence the name "Badlands."

Crater Lake, relic of an ancient volcanic explosion, is rimmed by fifteen miles of sheer cliffs two thousand feet high and as jagged in outline as the edges of a broken bottle. Nearly round and more than five miles across, the lake is more than a mile above sea level on the crest of the Cascade Range in Oregon—an expanse of water so still and so remarkably pure that it looks as deep and clean and blue as the stratosphere. An eerie stillness seems to trap and intensify the mountain silence. Strangely, after a short time one's ears begin to ring as if deafened by reverberations of the cataclysm which consumed a mountaintop.

But what captures the imagination is the specter of that vanished mountain, for it is impossible to admire the lake without reconstructing the phenomenon which created it. While Crater Lake plays tricks with the ears and its diamond brilliance is a feast for the eyes, the mind is busy recreating an event which took place about six thousand years ago.

The geology of the spectacular cliffs surrounding Crater Lake provides clues to the structure of the twelve-thousand-foot-high peak known as Mount Mazama, the name conferred on the area by local Indians long after the mountain was destroyed. Its complex and roughly conical shape was brought into being over hundreds of thousands of years by successive lava flows from the volcano. These layers can still be seen as clearly as the age rings of a log. Entire sections of cliff comprise funnel-shaped masses of lava showing where the side vents opened in the mature mountain, oozing molten rock down the slopes and indicating that the mountain did not have the geometric outlines of nearby Mount St. Helens and Mount Hood. Harder materials, forced from below into cracks in the mountainside, remain now as buttresses, jutting out sharply and in a variety of colors. These variegations, vents and buttresses give a clear idea of the shape and size of Mount Mazama.

The U-shaped dips in the skyline around Crater Lake show where the side of the mountain was scoured into deep valleys and gorges by glaciers. Scratches in the glacier-polished rocks show the extent and direction of glaciers during successive ice ages. When the explosion occurred, the glaciers were in their last period of retreat. The events which reduced the mountain to rubble took place within only a matter of days.

The tribes of Indians inhabiting the forests and tundra of the Northwest must have stood in awe and fear as the great clouds of white-hot ash boiled miles high from the top of the mountain. Carried by the wind, it melted glaciers and set forests alight where it fell, covering five thousand square miles to a depth of up to twenty feet. Dust covered the landscape for six hundred miles to the north, far into present-day British Columbia. In modern times, only the destruc-

Crater Lake

tion of Krakatoa in the East Indies, in 1883, bears comparison, and that was heard three thousand miles away. The Mount Mazama explosion would probably have been heard as far away as Hawaii, Lake Erie and the Gulf Coast.

So much material, over half its height, was blasted from the mountain that the reservoir deep inside could not replenish itself in time to prevent the creation of a vast cavern. Almost eight cubic miles of solid rock shattered into fragments and slid with a crescendo of noise and rising dust into the hole beneath.

When the dust settled, a four-thousand-foot-deep caldera had formed in place of a mile-high peak. The rain and melting snow half-filled the crater to the point where evaporation and seepage balanced precipitation. Later, a minor eruption formed Wizard Island, a small cone of cinders in the lake. The lake maintains a constant depth of 1,932 feet, making it one of the deepest lakes in the world. Some algae at the lake bottom are the only natural life there. Rainbow trout and kokanee salmon were recently introduced into the lake, but the water proved too pure for them.

Geologically, the great Mount Mazama volcano is now extinct, its energy expended. Crater Lake remains, beautiful and silent. During most of the year the craggy terrain around the lake is covered by deep drifts of snow, the dazzling white enriching the vivid blue of the water. The reflection, blurred here and there by soft breezes, seems unreal, and the imagination is easily stirred to a vivid recreation of the holocaust that consumed a mountain.

John Dyson

Fallen leaves do not rustle underfoot; they crumple like wet paper. Broken branches bend or tear, but do not snap. Soggy twigs fold rather than crack. It is a wonderland where delicate ferns and mosses flourish in the shade of some of the world's mightiest trees— an enchanting, mysterious and magical wilderness that is quite unlike any other place on earth.

The Olympic rain forest covers three deep, glacier-formed valleys on the western slopes of the Olympic Mountains, near the coast of Washington. Technically, a rain forest is an area that receives more than eighty inches of rain annually. Here the moisture-laden Pacific Ocean airstreams are deflected upward so sharply by the mountains that they are condensed by the cold air to form an astonishing yearly average of 142 inches of rain.

Olympic Rain Forest

The characteristic of a true rain forest is perpetual dampness. The sodden, still atmosphere creates a natural greenhouse, where ferns, mosses and lichens cover every twig, branch and stump. Clubmosses trail from branches in long, wispy beards. Velvety mosses quilt the rough bark of tall conifers and shroud the pulpy fibers of rotting logs. Ferns form crowns high up in the trees and tiny toadstools grow in the dark, damp hollows of tree stumps.

It is more like an underwater world than a forest. Short flashes of sunlight break through the green canopy of trees like reflections on the sea, while the light at ground level is a dim aquarium-green. The feathery mosses resemble wafting seaweed, and the impression of being underwater is heightened by the sensation of weightlessness one has when walking on the thick-sprung mattress of spongy mosses, ferns and creepers.

The Olympic rain forest is unique, not only in its atmosphere but also as a phenomenon of nature. It is the world's only true coniferous rain forest and the only temperate rain forest. Unlike all other rain forests, which are found in the tropics, it is not a dense tangle of vines and creepers because browsing black-tailed deer and Roosevelt elk keep the undergrowth under control. Consequently, the forest is a delight to walk through, and wildlife abounds. Tiny Douglas squirrels and snowshoe hares scurry about, cougars and coyotes stalk their prey, beavers feed on

the bark of alders along the banks of dashing rivers, and black bears fish for salmon and steelhead trout. The distant hammering of a woodpecker or the cackling of a jay emphasizes the stillness, and there is always the steady, muffled rustle of water dripping down from leaf to leaf, even when it is not actually raining.

Bastions of the forest are its great trees, which average two hundred and fifty feet in height, some topping three hundred feet. The largest known specimens of four species—western hemlock, Douglas fir, red alder and western red cedar—are found in or near its borders. Strangely, their roots go down only three or four feet, so eventually the giants are toppled by the winter gales, often gusting to more than one hundred miles an hour, that funnel up the forest valleys.

After a tree falls, the process of decay begins. This decay is a particularly potent force on which the renewal of the rain forest depends. Within five years the fallen tree is covered by a dense mat of moss and lichen. Then ferns take root; and, in the water-softened bark of the dead tree, seedlings of bigger trees spring up as a slowly developing forest in miniature. A twenty-year-old spruce might be only a foot high, yet its roots may have to go down twenty or thirty feet to reach the ground. Once it "pegs in," however, the tree shoots up, reaching its full height in about one hundred and fifty years.

A tree may live as long as eight hundred years, and it may be as many years again before all traces of it have disappeared. Nearly all the trees in the forest have begun life as seedlings on "nurse" logs and, in one of the remarkable features of the rain forest, have grown to create long and grand colonnades. At first the rain forest seems as haphazard as any jungle, but one soon realizes that each tree aligns perfectly with several of its neighbors. Often one can sight, through tunnels below, the arched roots of several trees in succession, showing where the nurse log they shared has completely rotted away.

Every tree soon collects its own colony of mosses, lichens and ferns, called epiphytes because they are supported by other plants. One tree can carry as many as forty species of these delicate plants.

The imagination can run riot in a place such as this, yet the forest is neither oppressive nor frightening. It is mysterious but not ghostly, damp but not chilling. It is silent—yet alive with faint whispers.

John Dyson

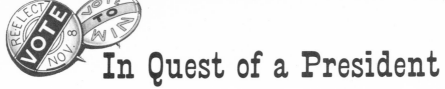

In Quest of a President

Every four years, Americans go to the polls to elect a President and Vice President. For many voters, the choice is simply a matter of deciding between the Democrats and the Republicans. Although third parties have surfaced from time to time—Theodore Roosevelt's Bull Moose, which split from the GOP in 1912, for example, and George Wallace's American Independent Party in 1968—American national politics still work basically within the two-party system.

The two-party tradition goes back to the early years of the nation's history. Although the Founding Fathers were suspicious of parties and even ignored them altogether in drafting the Constitution, Americans formed political alliances in the late 1700s to win elections and influence the policies of the government.

In 1796, George Washington had refused to run for a third term, so the election that year was a party contest between a Federalist, John Adams, and a Democratic-Republican, Thomas Jefferson.

By the end of Washington's administration, there were two fairly well defined political groups in the country. The Federalists, including Washington, Hamilton, Adams and their supporters, were nationalist in their outlook and favored a strong federal government. The Anti-Federalists, led by Thomas Jefferson and his supporters, tended to be more isolationist and favored less activity by the federal government.

In the years that followed, parties developed as Democratic-Republicans (later Democrats) and National Republicans, from 1769 to 1815; Democrats and Whigs, from 1835 to 1852; and Democrats and Republicans, from 1854 until today.

Political parties act somewhat as "brokers" who help to translate the wishes of the people into government policy. Parties help to explain complex issues, and they bring a kind of necessary order to the chaotic process of choosing among a multitude of candidates. Through primary elections, caucuses and conventions, party members decide which candidates to endorse in the general election, and they help to narrow the choice for the voting public.

A major political party must attract as many voters as possible. So parties are built on a broad philosophical base, and their platforms must appeal to a great variety of voters. Differences in the two major American parties seem to center around political philosophy. Republicans are generally considered to be more conservative; their platform in 1976, for instance, focused on reduced federal spending, more local control, and less governmental interference in the economy. That same year the Democratic platform favored greater use of the government's powers to promote full employment, relieve poverty and enforce civil rights legislation.

The final vote for the Presidency comes from the Electoral College, a concept dating back to 1787 when the Founding Fathers were drafting the Constitution. Debating how a President should be chosen, they decided that each state would choose wise and educated men to vote for all the people. The groups of electors came to be known as the Electoral College.

Political parties began to form by the election of 1796, and they took on the job of nominating presidential candidates. Electors were presented with party-supported candidates to choose from, and gradually more and more people were allowed to vote.

By 1828, in all but two of the twenty-four states, the electors were chosen by popular elections rather than state legislatures. Each party named electors who would vote for its presidential candidate, and the electors of the winning party almost automatically cast the state's electoral votes for their party's candidate.

The choice of a President has come closer to the common people than the Founding Fathers had intended. Although the Electoral College is considered to be an echo of the voice of the people, the concept has been criticized through the years, and various suggestions have been advanced for correcting its faults. Changing the structure of the College would require a Constitutional amendment, however.

Selected party members, or delegates, gather from all over the country every four years to attend the national conventions that serve four basic needs: to nominate the two top candidates, to adopt a national party platform, to govern the party, and to serve as an exciting, enthusiastic campaign rally.

The Presidency has grown so complex that a good many people wonder if any mortal can adequately fill the office. Nonetheless, the quest for this "splendid misery" reaches its culmination every four years in the national conventions where two men are singled out for the highest offices in the land.

Few of the thirty-eight former Presidents, however, had anything good to say about the office. Thomas Jefferson commented, "Never did a prisoner released from his chains feel such relief as I shall on shaking off the shackles of power." Truman remarked that "Being a President is like riding a tiger. A man has to keep riding or be swallowed." And Gen. William Tecumseh Sherman, who soundly resisted a "Draft Sherman" movement, made this sharp comment: "If forced to choose between the penitentiary and the White House for four years, I would say the penitentiary, thank you."

This year, the Republicans will hold their convention during the week of July 14 in Detroit. Democrats will gather at Madison Square Garden in New York City beginning August 11.

Republican delegates and their families can savor Detroit's historic flavor. The city was settled in 1701 by the French and named "d'etroit" or city "of straits," a reference to the twenty-seven-mile Detroit River that connects Lakes Erie and St. Clair. Belle Isle, an island park in the middle of the river, offers visitors an Aquarium, a Children's Zoo, and an Urban Nature Center.

Renaissance Center, a new civic center complex on the riverfront, is the largest privately financed development in the country. Although Detroit is thought of as the "Motor City," there are attractions other than those connected with the manufacture of automobiles. Many points of interest reflect Detroit's maritime connection, such as Old Mariner's Church and the Dossin Great Lakes Museum of Belle Isle.

Convention-goers can choose from several fine restaurants along the river or atop sky-high revolving rooftops downtown. Good ethnic restaurants offer Greek and Chinese food; some delegates might choose to eat, appropriately enough, at the Caucus Club.

Nearby Dearborn is a feast of American history. Greenfield Village offers Historic Houses, Suwanee Park and Island, the Thomas A. Edison Buildings and the Village Green. The Henry Ford Museum in Dearborn features the American Decorative Arts Galleries, Henry Ford Exhibits, Mechanical Arts Hall, and memorabilia in the Street of Early American Shops.

When the Democrats get together in the Big Apple in August, they'll find such an overwhelming variety of diversions that the choices are staggering. The three-hundred-foot-high Statue of Liberty, dominating the approach to the city's harbor, has been welcoming the "huddled masses yearning to breathe free" since 1885.

New York is a city of spectacular museums. The American Museum of Natural History is the largest in the world, with more than forty acres of floor space. The Whitney holds a vast collection of contemporary art; the Metropolitan Museum houses a collection of more than a million art objects that span the entire five thousand years of civilized human culture, and the Cloisters at Fort Tyron Park offer a splendid collection of medieval art. The Guggenheim, designed by Frank Lloyd Wright, holds a permanent collection of more than four thousand works of modern art.

Delegates will be awed by New York's skyscraper skyline—the Empire State Building, the art-deco style Chrysler Building, Rockefeller Center, the United Nations Building, and the twin towers of the 1302-foot tall World Trade Center. When the day's convention business is finished, the lights of Broadway will lead visitors to the best in legitimate American theater.

In both cities, after the applause and the balloons and the speeches and the hoopla, delegates will nominate their party's candidates.

Bea Bourgeois

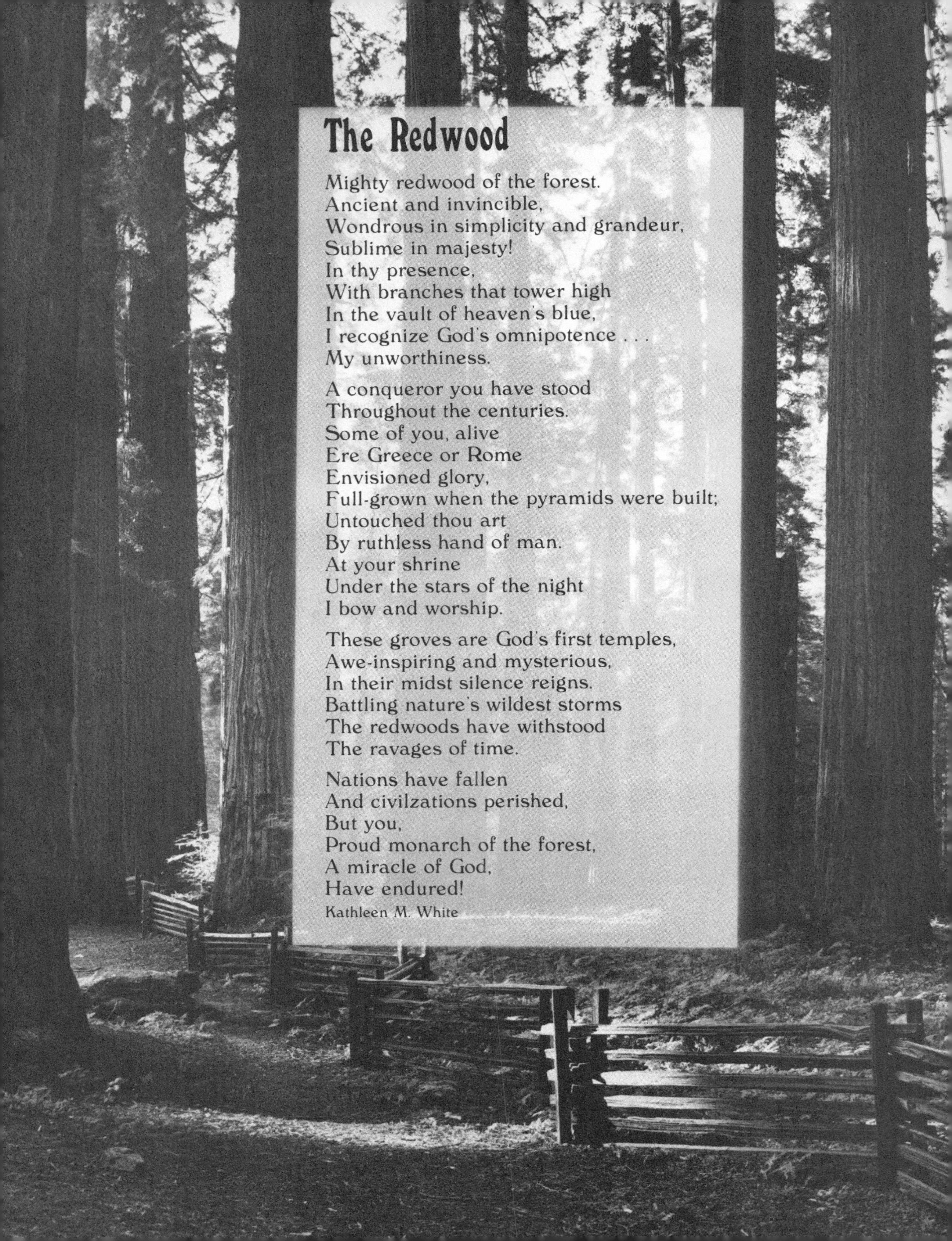

The Redwood

Mighty redwood of the forest.
Ancient and invincible,
Wondrous in simplicity and grandeur,
Sublime in majesty!
In thy presence,
With branches that tower high
In the vault of heaven's blue,
I recognize God's omnipotence . . .
My unworthiness.

A conqueror you have stood
Throughout the centuries.
Some of you, alive
Ere Greece or Rome
Envisioned glory,
Full-grown when the pyramids were built;
Untouched thou art
By ruthless hand of man.
At your shrine
Under the stars of the night
I bow and worship.

These groves are God's first temples,
Awe-inspiring and mysterious,
In their midst silence reigns.
Battling nature's wildest storms
The redwoods have withstood
The ravages of time.

Nations have fallen
And civilzations perished,
But you,
Proud monarch of the forest,
A miracle of God,
Have endured!

Kathleen M. White

The sunshine falls in glory through the colossal spires and crowns, each a symbol of health and strength, the noble shafts faithfully upright like pillars of temples, upholding a roof of infinite, leafy, interlacing arches and fretted skylights.

John Muir

Redwood Sentinels

I feel their iron bark and know
These redwoods stand to testify
That long after man has known his day
Their lofty arms will brush the sky.

Their branches meet above my head,
Where silent, dusky green
Of shadows and the sigh of winds
Are lonely and serene.

I make a prayer to God
To praise his plan:
How tall, the redwood . . .
How small is man.

Helen Virden

Isles of the Sea

Agnes Davenport Bond

Isles of the sea,
Isles of the sea,
Today, they are
Fresh in my memory,
A land of romance,
Where beauty lies,
Under the clearest
Of sapphire skies,
Where the scent is sweet
Of Hawaiian flowers,
And the sunlight streams
Through the fitful showers.
And the salty tang
Of the ocean sweeps.
Here lavishly bloom
All shrubs and trees;
And fragrance is wafted
On the breeze.
A country of color,
Of splendor, and thrills,
Of seashore and mountains,
Of valleys and hills.

How enchanting these crossroads
Far out on the sea!
And their lure of adventure
Is calling me.
I want to go back
To Aloha land,
And lie again
On the sea-washed sand,
And to hear again,
At the channel buoy,
The sweet, sad strains
Of "Aloha Oe."
Isles of the sea,
Isles of the sea,
Treasured today
In my memory.

Alaska Highway

The 1,422-mile Alaska Highway is the only road connecting Alaska with Canadian and United States road systems. Built during World War II as a military supply route, the highway cost $140 million and has a mostly gravel surface.

Eiffel Tower

Designed for the 1889 exposition by Gustave Eiffel, the Eiffel Tower rises 984 feet above the city of Paris. About 6,400 metric tons of iron and steel make up the tower, which houses restaurants, elevators, areas for experimentation and a weather station.

The Seven Wonders
of the

Golden Gate Bridge

Joseph B. Strauss designed the 8,981-foot-long Golden Gate Bridge, which connects northern California to the peninsula of San Francisco. This spectacular suspension bridge, containing a six-lane road and sidewalks, is supported by two cables, 36½ inches in diameter.

R. Adair

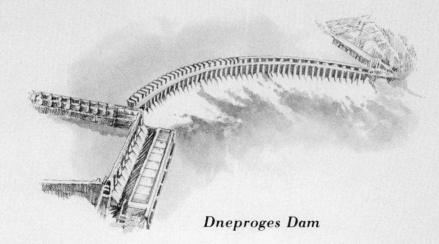

Dneproges Dam

The Dneproges Dam on the Dnepr River supplies hydroelectric power for a majority of southern Russia's mines and industries. The 5,000-foot-long concrete structure holds back 1,600,000 cubic yards of water used to generate 650,000 kilowatts of electricity.

Empire State Building

New York City's Empire State Building rises 1,472 feet, including 102 stories and a television tower. The fifty-year-old skyscraper houses about 10,000 tenants and has over 1½ million visitors annually.

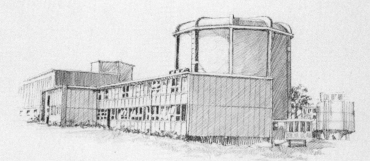

Atomic Energy Research Establishment

Modern World

One of the world's major scientific laboratories is the Atomic Energy Research Establishment at Harwell, England. Experimental facilities, including several large particle accelerators and six research reactors, enable researchers to study all aspects of atomic energy.

Suez Canal

The man-made Suez Canal waterway in Egypt extends nearly 100 miles across the Isthmus of Suez, joining the Mediterranean and Red seas. The canal has been widened and deepened several times since its construction in 1869. Currently 46 feet deep and 390 feet wide at the surface, the canal is, for the most part, limited to one-lane traffic.

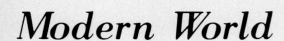

PHOTOS THAT SAY, "LOOK AT ME"

Successful photography depends upon more than technique, for another requirement is an awareness of aesthetics. Great photographs depend more upon the principles of beauty than they do upon a mastery of the technical aspects of photography. What is the main difference between a mere snapshot and an outstanding photo? An understanding of the answer to this question can help make travel pictures a joy for all to behold.

Let us suppose someone were to travel to Hawaii and take a picture at the beach. What would the photo look like? Would it contain a hodgepodge of sunbathers lying about the beach in helter-skelter fashion, with palm trees jutting in and out of the picture? If so, it would be an example of one of the capital sins of aesthetics: disorganization. In order to become meaningful, the various elements of a photograph should not be brought together in an entirely arbitrary manner, but should be arranged into a harmonious whole. For an example of a photograph which is carefully organized and illustrates some of the basic axioms of good composition, let us take a look at the photo on the opposite page.

First of all, the elements of this travel picture are arranged in a meaningful way. The picture seems to shout, "Hawaii," for one glimpse is all that is needed to discern its location. Everything one needs to know in order to identify the locale is there: Diamond Head, palm trees, blue sky and ocean, beach and bathers, sailboats and hotels. And yet, the photo is not at all crowded.

This brings us to our second principle of good pictures: simplicity. It is generally true that the smaller the number of elements in a picture, the better. The trick is to use just enough elements to deliver your message. Of course, if you want to show how crowded a particular beach may be, include plenty of people, but do not include anything irrelevant. The rule of simplicity extends to design and color. In other words, the simpler the design and the fewer the colors, the better the picture will be, except of course, when the theme specifically deals with complexity of design or color.

The next design element is as simple as they come: framing the subject. Note how the innermost trees frame Diamond Head, the boats, and the first couple; next, how the pair of trees on the right frame the standing couple. At the same time, the outermost trees serve as a border, unifying all of the elements to form a single meaningful picture.

Another attribute of the photograph is balance. In the foreground, there are four trees and four people, and both trees and people are divided into groups of two. In addition to this rhythmical repetition of elements, the position of the horizon also affects the overall balance of the picture. A successful scenic usually has a high or low horizon, and the picture grows increasingly less appealing as the horizon approaches the exact center of the composition.

Still another characteristic of all good pictures is mood. That is, the ability to convey an emotion. What emotion or mood does our example photo communicate, and how do the various elements of the picture help deliver the message? The mood is tranquility. Note how this feeling seems to permeate the scene: both couples are at rest, the boats are moored; there are no strong waves visible; the palm leaves seem to indicate the absence of any wind. In other words, the scene is full of inactivity.

Additionally, the long shadows of the trees hint that it is nearing the end of the day, a time of rest. Again, the predominant color is blue, which psychologically conveys the feeling of peace. Finally, because the mere name "Hawaii" conjures up an image of a place to relax, the very elements which identify the location of the photograph assist in conveying the mood of tranquility.

Although these many points are not obvious at the conscious level of our minds, they are nevertheless picked up by the subconscious (the seat of our emotions), and are thereby worthy of consideration. The lesson is clear: for better travel pictures, think before you shoot; take time to organize.

Chuck Gallozzi

Article and photograph opposite
Courtesy of *Photo Life* Magazine
For subscription information
Write 230 - 144 Front Street West
Toronto, Ontario M5J 1G2

Around the World in Eighty Days
Jules Verne

This abridged version has been prepared
especially for Ideals
by Norma Barnes

Mr. Phileas Fogg lived, in 1872, at No. 7, Saville Row, Burlington Gardens. . . . Was [he] rich? Undoubtedly. But those who knew him best could not imagine how he had made his fortune. . . . He was . . . the least communicative of men. . . . His daily habits were quite open to observation; but whatever he did was so exactly the same thing that he had always done before that the wits of the curious were fairly puzzled.

Phileas Fogg was not known to have either wife or children, . . . relatives or near friends. . . . He lived alone in his house in Saville Row. . . . The mansion, though not sumptuous, was exceedingly comfortable. . . .

. . .

A rap . . . sounded on the door . . . A young man of thirty advanced and bowed. "You are a Frenchman, I believe," asked Phileas Fogg.

"Jean Passepartout, . . ." replied the newcomer.

"You are well recommended to me; I hear a good report of you. . . . What time is it?" Mr. Fogg asked.

"Twenty-two minutes after eleven," returned Passepartout, drawing an enormous silver watch from the depths of his pocket.

"You are too slow," said Mr. Fogg.

"Pardon me, Monsieur, it is impossible—"

"You are four minutes too slow. No matter; it's enough to mention the error. Now from this moment, twenty-nine minutes after eleven A.M., this Wednesday, October 2, you are in my service."

. . .

A Daring Wager

Several members of the Reform Club came in and drew up to the fireplace, where a coal fire was steadily burning. They were Mr. Fogg's usual partners at whist . . . , all rich and highly respectable personages.

"Well, Ralph," said Thomas Flanagan, "what about that robbery?"

"I hope we may put our hands on the robber. Skillful detectives have been sent to all the principal ports of America and the Continent, and he'll be a clever fellow if he slips through their fingers."

"But have you got the robber's description?" asked Stuart.

"In the first place, he is no robber at all," returned Ralph, positively. . . .

"The *Daily Telegraph* says that he is a gentleman."

It was Phileas Fogg, whose head now emerged from behind his newspaper, who made this remark. He bowed to his friends and entered into the conversation . . .

There were real grounds for supposing, as the *Daily Telegraph* said, that the thief did not belong to a professional band. On the day of the robbery a well-dressed gentleman of polished manners, with a well-to-do air, had been observed going to and fro in the paying-room, where the crime was committed.

"I maintain," said Stuart, "that the chances are in favor of the thief, who must be a shrewd fellow."

"Well, but where can he fly to?" asked Ralph. "No country is safe for him."

"Pshaw!"

"Oh, I don't know that. The world is big enough."

"It was once," said Phileas Fogg, in a low tone.

. . . "What do you mean by 'once'? Has the world grown smaller?"

"Certainly," returned Ralph. "I agree with Mr. Fogg. The world has grown smaller, since a man can now go round it ten times more quickly than a hundred years ago."

"In eighty days," interrupted Phileas Fogg.

. . . "I'd like to see you do it in eighty days. . . . I would wager four thousand pounds that such a journey . . . is impossible. . . ."

. . ."All right," said Mr. Fogg and, turning to the others, he continued, "I have a deposit of twenty thousand at Baring's which I will willingly risk upon it. . . . Do you accept?"

"We accept," replied Messrs. Stuart, Fallentin, Sullivan, Flanagan, and Ralph, after consulting each other.

A Beginning

. . . By eight o'clock Passepartout had packed the modest carpetbag containing the wardrobes of his master and himself; then, still troubled in mind, he carefully shut the door of his room, and descended to Mr. Fogg.

. . .

Mr. Fogg and his servant seated themselves in a first-class carriage at twenty minutes before nine; five minutes later the whistle screamed, and the train slowly glided out of the station. . .

A Suspicion

. . . The commissioner of police was sitting in his office at nine o'clock one evening, when the following telegraphic dispatch was put into his hands:

Suez to London

Rowan, Commissioner of Police, Scotland Yard: I've found the bank robber, Phileas Fogg. Send without delay warrant of arrest to Bombay.

Fix, Detective

The mysterious habits of Phileas Fogg were recalled; his solitary ways, his sudden departure; and it seemed clear that, in undertaking a tour round the world on the pretext of a wager, he had had no other end in view than to elude the detectives and throw them off his track.

. . .

A Dubious Friendship

Detective Fix joined Passepartout, who was lounging and looking about on the quay. . . . "Well, my friend . . . you are looking about you?"

"Yes, but we travel so fast that I seem to be journeying in a dream."

"You are in a great hurry, then?"

"I am not, but my master is . . . Above all," said Passepartout, "don't let me lose the steamer."

"You have plenty of time; it's only twelve o'clock."

Passepartout pulled out his big watch. "Twelve!" he exclaimed. "Why it's only eight minutes before ten."

"Your watch is slow."

"My watch? It doesn't vary five minutes in the year; it's a perfect chronometer."

"I see how it is," said Fix. "You have kept London time, which is two hours behind that of Suez. You ought to regulate your watch at noon in each country."

"I regulate my watch? Never!"

"Well, then, it will not agree with the sun."

"So much the worse for the sun, Monsieur. The sun will be [wr]ong, then!" And the worthy fellow returned the watch to its fob [wi]th a defiant gesture.

. . . Passepartout and Fix got into the habit of chatting together, [th]e latter making it a point to gain the worthy man's confidence, [t]he unsuspecting] Passepartout, mentally pronouncing Fix the [be]st of good fellows.

. . . What was Phileas Fogg doing all this time? He made his four [he]arty meals every day, regardless of the most persistent rolling [an]d pitching on the part of the steamer; and he played whist [in]defatigably. . . .

The Journey Continues

. . . The *Mongolia* was due at Bombay on the 22nd; she arrived [o]n the 20th. This was a gain to Phileas Fogg of two days since his [d]eparture from London, and he calmly entered the fact in the [i]tinerary, in the columns of gains.

The passengers of the *Mongolia* went ashore at half-past four [P.]M.; at exactly eight the train would start for Calcutta.

. . .

A Heroic Adventure

. . . The train stopped, at eight o'clock, in the midst of a glade [s]ome fifteen miles beyond Rothal, where there were several [b]ungalows and workmen's cabins. The conductor, passing along [th]e carriages, shouted, "Passengers will get out here!" . . .

. . . The railway came to a termination at this point. The papers [it seemed] were like some watches, which have a way of getting [to]o fast, and had been premature in their announcement of the [c]ompletion of the line. . . .

. . .

Mr. Fogg and Sir Francis Cromarty, after searching the village [f]rom end to end, came back without having found any means of [c]onveyance.

"I shall go afoot," said Phileas Fogg.

Passepartout had been looking about him and, after a moment's [h]esitation, said, "Monsieur, I think I have found our means of [c]onveyance."

"What?"

"An elephant! An elephant that belongs to an Indian who lives [b]ut a hundred steps from here."

"Let's go and see the elephant," replied Mr. Fogg. . . .

Phileas Fogg proposed to purchase the animal outright, [and] [a]t two thousand pounds the Indian yielded.

"What a price, good heaven!" cried Passepartout, "for an [e]lephant!"

. . . At two o'clock the [party] entered a thick forest which [e]xtended several miles; [the guide] preferred to travel under [c]over of the woods. They had not as yet had any unpleasant [e]ncounters, and the journey seemed on the point of being [s]uccessfully accomplished, when the elephant, becoming restless, [s]uddenly stopped.

"A procession of Brahmans is coming this way. We must prevent their seeing us, if possible." . . .

. . . Some Brahmans, [were approaching] clad in all the [s]umptuousness of Oriental apparel, and leading a woman who [f]altered at every step. This woman was young, and as fair as a European. Her head and neck, shoulders, ears, arms, hands, and [t]oes, were loaded down with jewels and gems, with bracelets, [e]arrings, and rings. . . .

. . . Sir Francis watched the procession with a sad countenance, and, turning to the guide, said, "A suttee."

The Parsee nodded, and put his finger to his lips. . . .

. . . Phileas Fogg had heard what Sir Francis said, and, as soon as the procession had disappeared, asked, "What is a 'suttee'?"

"A suttee," returned the general, "is a human sacrifice, but a voluntary one. The woman you have just seen will be burned tomorrow at the dawn of day."

"And the corpse?" asked Mr. Fogg.

"Is that of the prince, her husband," said the guide; "an independent Raja of Bundelcund." . . .

. . . The guide shook his head several times, and now said, "The sacrifice which will take place tomorrow at dawn is not a voluntary one."

"How do you know?"

"Everybody knows about this affair in Bundelcund."

"But the wretched creature did not seem to be making any resistance," observed Sir Francis.

"That was because they had intoxicated her with fumes of hemp and opium" . . .

. . . Mr. Fogg stopped him, and, turning to Sir Francis Cromarty, said, "Suppose we save this woman."

"Save the woman, Mr. Fogg!"

"I have yet twelve hours to spare; I can devote them to that."

"Why, you are a man of heart!"

"Sometimes," replied Phileas Fogg, quietly, "when I have the time." . . .

. . .

The hours passed, and the lighter shades now announced the approach of day, though it was not yet light. This was the moment.

Phileas Fogg and his companions mingled in the rear ranks of the crowd; and in two minutes they reached the banks of the stream and stopped fifty paces from the pyre, upon which still lay the raja's corpse. In the semi-obscurity they saw the victim, quite senseless, stretched out beside her husband's body. Then a torch was brought, and the wood, soaked with oil, instantly took fire.

At this moment Sir Francis and the guide seized Phileas Fogg, who, in an instant of mad generosity, was about to rush upon the pyre. But he had quickly pushed them aside, when the whole scene suddenly changed. A cry of terror arose. The whole multitude prostrated themselves, terror-stricken, on the ground.

The old raja was not dead, then, since he rose of a sudden, like a specter, took up his wife in his arms, and descended from the pyre in the midst of the clouds of smoke, which only heightened his ghostly appearance.

continued

It was Passepartout who had . . . slipped upon the pyre . . . and delivered the young woman from death.

A moment after, all four of the party had disappeared in the woods, and the elephant was bearing them away at a rapid pace. But the cries and the noise, and a ball which whizzed through Phileas Fogg's hat, apprised them that the trick had been discovered.

The old raja's body, indeed, now appeared upon the pyre; and the priests, recovered from their terror, perceived that an abduction had taken place. They hastened into the forest, followed by the soldiers, who fired a volley after the fugitives; but the latter rapidly increased the distance between them, and ere long found themselves beyond the reach of the bullets and arrows.

. . . Soon after, Phileas Fogg, Sir Francis Cromarty, and Passepartout, were installed in a carriage with Aouda (the young woman whom they had rescued). . . .

Phileas Fogg . . . offered . . . to escort her to Hong Kong, where she might remain safely until the affair was hushed up—an offer which she eagerly and gratefully accepted. She had a relation, who was one of the principal merchants of Hong Kong, . . .

A Gracious Offer

[In Hong Kong] Mr. Fog repaired to the Exchange, where, he made the inquiry, only to learn that [Aouda's relative] had left China two years before, and, retiring from business with an immense fortune, had taken up his residence in Europe—in Holland, the broker thought.

Aouda at first said nothing. she passed her hand across her forehead, and reflected a few moments. Then, in her sweet, soft voice, she said, "What ought I to do, Mr. Fogg?"

"It is very simple," responded the gentleman. "Go on to Europe."

Across a Vast Continent

. . . On the 3rd of December, the "General Grant" entered the bay of the Golden Gate and reached San Francisco.

Mr. Fogg had neither gained nor lost a single day.

. . . The train left Oakland station at six o'clock. It was already night, cold and cheerless, the heavens being overcast with clouds which seemed to threaten snow.

. . . About twelve o'clock, a troup of ten or twelve thousand head of buffalo encumbered the track. The locomotive, slackening its speed, tried to clear the way with its cowcatcher; but the mass of animals was too great. The buffaloes marched along with a tranquil gait, uttering now and then deafening bellowings. There was no use in interrupting them, for, having taken a particular

direction, nothing can moderate and change their course; it is a torrent of living flesh which no dam could contain.

. . . The train pursued its course, without interruption.

. . . Suddenly savage cries resounded in the air, accompanied by reports which certainly did not issue from the car where [they] were. The reports continued in front and the whole length of the train. Cries of terror proceeded from the interior of the cars.

Colonel Proctor and Mr. Fogg, revolvers in hand, . . . rushed forward where the noise was most clamorous. They then perceived that the train was attacked by a band of Sioux.

The Sioux were armed with guns, from which came the reports, to which the passengers, who were almost all armed, responded by revolver shots.

Fort Kearney station, where there was a garrison, was only two miles distant; but that once passed, the Sioux would be masters of the train between Fort Kearney and the station beyond.

[The train continued to roll.] The conductor was fighting beside Mr. Fogg, when he was shot and fell. At the same moment he cried, "Unless the train is stopped in five minutes, we are lost!"

"Stay, Monsieur," said Passepartout; "I will go."

Carried on by the force already acquired, the train still moved for several minutes; but the brakes were worked, and at last they stopped, less than a hundred feet from Kearney station.

The soldiers of the fort, attracted by the shots, hurried up; the Sioux had not expected them, and decamped in a body before the train entirely stopped.

. . .

Phileas Fogg found himself twenty hours behind time. He examined a curious vehicle, a kind of frame on two long beams, a little raised in front like the runners of a sledge, and upon which there was room for five or six persons. . . .

What a journey! The travellers, huddled close together, could not speak for the cold, intensified by the rapidity at which they were going. . . .

A train was ready to start when Mr. Fogg and his party reached the station, and they only had time to get into the cars.

. . . At last the Hudson came into view; and at a quarter-past eleven in the evening of the 11th, the train stopped in the station on the right bank of the river, before the very pier of the Cunard line.

The "China," for Liverpool, had started three quarters of an hour before!

A Mutiny

[Phileas Fogg] seemed about to give up all hope, when he espied a trading vessel getting ready for departure. . . .

"Will you carry me and three other persons to Liverpool?"

"No! I am setting out for Bordeaux. . . ."

"Well, will you carry me to Bordeaux?"

"No, not if you paid me two hundred dollars."

"I offer you two thousand."

"Apiece?"

"Apiece."

. . . "I start at nine o'clock," said Captain Speedy, simply. . . . .

"We will be on board at nine o'clock," replied, no less simply, Mr. Fogg.

. . . They were on board when the "Henrietta" made ready to weigh anchor. . . .

At noon the next day . . . Captain Speedy . . . was shut up in his cabin under lock and key. . . .

Phileas Fogg wished to go to Liverpool, but the captain would not carry him there. . . . [So he] had so shrewdly managed with his banknotes that the sailors and stokers . . . went over to him in a body. . . .

On the 18th of December, the engineer . . . announced that the coal would give out in the course of the day.

. . .

"I have sent for you, [Captain]," continued Mr. Fogg, "to ask you to sell me your vessel."

"No! By all the devils, no!"

"But I shall be obliged to burn her."

"Burn the 'Henrietta'!"

"Yes; at least the upper part of her. The coal has given out."

"Burn my vessel!" cried Captain Speedy, who could scarcely pronounce the words. "A vessel worth fifty thousand dollars!"

"Here are sixty thousand," replied Phileas Fogg.

. . .

Phileas Fogg at last disembarked on the Liverpool quay, at twenty minutes before twelve, December 21st. He was only six hours distant from London.

The Final Delay

But at this moment Fix came up, put his hand upon Mr. Fogg's shoulder, and, showing his warrant, said, "You are really Phileas Fogg?"

"I am."

"I arrest you in the Queen's name!"

Phileas Fogg was in prison. He had been shut up in the Custom House, and he was to be transferred to London the next day.

The Custom House clock struck one. Mr. Fogg observed that his watch was two hours too fast.

Two hours! Admitting that he was at this moment taking an express train, he could reach London and the Reform Club by a quarter before nine, p.m. His forehead slightly wrinkled.

The door swung open, and he saw Passepartout, Aouda, and Fix, who hurried towards him.

Fix was out of breath, and his hair was in disorder. He could not speak. "Sir," he stammered, "Sir—forgive me—a most-unfortunate resemblance—robber arrested three days ago—you—are free!"

Phileas Fogg was free!

Phileas Fogg then ordered a special train.

But . . . when Mr. Fogg stepped from the train at the terminus, all the clocks in London were striking ten minutes before nine.

Having made the tour of the world, he was behindhand five minutes. He had lost the wager!

All Is Lost?

Phileas Fogg returned home . . . took a chair, and sat down near the fireplace, opposite Aouda. No emotion was visible on his face. Fogg returned was exactly the Fogg who had gone away; there was the same calm, the same impassibility.

He sat several minutes without speaking; then, bending his eyes on Aouda, "Madam," said he, "will you pardon me for bringing you to England?"

"I, Mr. Fogg!" replied Aouda, checking the pulsations of her heart.

"Please let me finish," returned Mr. Fogg. "When I decided to bring you far away from the country which was so unsafe for you, I was rich, and counted on putting a portion of my fortune at your disposal; then your existence would have been free and happy. But now I am ruined. . . ."

"Mr. Fogg," said Aouda, rising, and seizing his hand, "do you wish at once a kinswoman and friend? Will you have me for your wife?"

Mr. Fogg shut his eyes for an instant, as if to avoid her look. When he opened them again, "I love you!" he said, simply. "Yes, by all that is holiest, I love you, and I am entirely yours!"

Passepartout was summoned.

. . .

A Victory

The five antagonists of Phileas Fogg had met in the great saloon of the club.

"Sixteen minutes to nine!" said John Sullivan, in a voice which betrayed his emotion.

One minute more, and the wager would be won.

At the fortieth second, nothing. At the fiftieth, still nothing.

At the fifty-fifth, a loud cry was heard in the street, followed by applause, hurrahs, and some fierce growls.

The players rose from their seats.

At the fifty-seventh second the door of the saloon opened; and the pendulum had not beat the sixtieth second when Phileas Fogg appeared, followed by an excited crowd who had forced their way through the club doors, and in his calm voice, said, "Here I am, gentlemen!"

Yes, Phileas Fogg in person.

The reader will remember that at five minutes past eight in the evening Passepartout had been sent by his master to engage the services of the Reverend Samuel Wilson.

He soon reached the clergyman's house, but found him not at home. Passepartout waited a good twenty minutes, and when he left the reverend gentleman, it was thirty-five minutes past eight. But in what a state he was!

Phileas Fogg had, without suspecting it, gained one day on his journey, and this merely because he had travelled constantly eastward; he would, on the contrary, have lost a day, had he gone in the opposite direction, that is, westward.

The Wealth of the World

That evening, Mr. Fogg, as tranquil as ever, said to Aouda, "Is our marriage still agreeable to you?"

"Mr. Fogg," replied she, "it is for me to ask that question. You were ruined, but now you are rich again."

"Pardon me, Madam; my fortune belongs to you."

What had he really gained by all this trouble? What had he brought back from this long and weary journey?

Nothing, say you? Perhaps so; nothing but a charming woman, who, strange as it may appear, made him the happiest of men!

Truly, would you not for less than that make the tour around the world?

Remember Paris? We savored petit fours
   At an outdoor café
And relaxed, inhaling the atmosphere.
   It was spring
And Paris had a lyrical loveliness,
   A loveliness almost ethereal . . .

Then we wandered along the Left Bank,
   Lingering at the Sorbonne and
Browsing through books and sketches
   Along the Boulevards Saint Michel
      And Saint Germain—
You bought me violets and held my hand,
   And we were alive with the wonder of Paris
      And ourselves . . .

One day we climbed up Montmartre,
   And there it was
The Cathedral of Sacre Coeur,
   Its white dome pink-gold in the sunset,
Imprinting itself upon us forever. . . .

We had a wonderful view of the city:
   The rooftops and lanes of Paris
Were before us—
   A palette of soft Utrillo colors

Remember Paris?

Lorice Fiani Mulhern

We strolled along the Champs Elysées
   In the shimmering sunlight
And kept falling in love with delightful Paris
   When, suddenly, it began to rain
      And thunder,
Melting trees and taxis and people together
   And arousing a symphony of discordant horns
Amid the driving slush and splatter.

One Sunday we sailed along the Seine,
   Marveling at the bridges and lamps
Of Paris (so many and so distinctive).
   We viewed the Cathedral of Notre Dame,
Hardly believing we were there—
   Remember?

Amid a scattering of treetops, chimneys
   And spires . . .
An artist nearby began folding his easel
   And a young boy walked along,
Playing his harmonica . . .

Such was Paris— Maxim's, the Louvre,
   The Eiffel Tower;
The sidewalk cafés athrong with people;
   The little side streets and shops,
The ride on the Metro . . .

All that fun and glamor,
   All that magnificent oldness and newness
Stirring and enrapturing us . . .
   Remember?

An Irish Mile

Maude Ludington Cain

Once, on a bright day, in a far, fairy isle,
I thought I would walk me an Irish mile—
An Irish mile was my morning desire,
So I took a gray road past a bog and a byre.
There was many a stone and many a stile,
But I would be going an Irish mile.
There were turf fires burning by benches, rough-hewn,
There was laughter, and lilt of an old Irish tune.
By sheep-cot and pen and a low, winding wall
I met an old grand'm with shillelagh and shawl;
I greeted a driver of donkey and cart,
To a blue-eyed colleen, sure, I near lost my heart.
And each spoke me cheery and gave me a smile
And bade me to tea and to rest for a while.
I heard barley sickles and smelled the ripe grain—
But never came I to the end of that lane.

Foot-weary at last and the sun going down
I came to a cottage close by to a town,
And said to a herder as I rested a while,
"Sure, 'tis long, friend, and long to the end of this mile."
He tipped his pipe ashes with a wave of his hand,
And replied, "Aye, it is that— but you understand
An Irish mile, darlin', is a mile and a bit—
And the bit, sure, is ever the most part of it . . ."
Oh, I can't be forgetting that slow Irish mile,
Where there's time for a chat and there's time for a smile;
Though on smooth roads and white roads I journey meanwhile
I fain would be going a far Irish mile—
A way-faring, gay-faring, sweet Irish mile.

Stonehenge: Monument of Mystery

Emmett Van Buskirk

Not far from Salisbury, England, and its great cathedral is the site of another imposing structure. On Salisbury Plain, Wiltshire, England, the massive stones of Stonehenge sit in majesty and mystery.

Stonehenge was probably built in several stages nearly four thousand years ago. Its construction occurred in what is referred to as the Neolithic Period (The New Stone Age). During this time man not only domesticated animals and plant forms, but also set aside and designed his own functional space in his world: established the beginnings of architecture. The materials used to construct many of these structures consisted of huge stones whose weight and size were so immense that the culture has been referred to as "megalithic." The name derives from the term "megalithic" given to describe the great stones.

I first saw Stonehenge one misty summer day, which only added to the mystery of this unique structure. My previous study did not prepare me for the awesome experience of walking among the massive stones. Even though there has been both natural and man-made destruction of the stones and their circular arrangement, the remains of Stonehenge still create an imposing sight.

Stonehenge is unique. There i nothing quite like it any other place in the world. Even from the earlies times visitors walked in amazemen through the site and wondered a its construction and function jus as I did.

Stonehenge is shaped in the form of a circle of huge stones known as a "cromlech." The outer boundary of this stone formation is a low circular bank and ditch about one hundred feet from the stones. The building itself consisted of an outer ring of large stones capped by a lintel (crossbeam) stone. Inside this was a circle of smaller stones and an inner horseshoe of five upright

and lintel pairs. Standing separately from the other stones is one which is thought to mark the summer solstice, June 21.

Nearly four thousand years ago man created this extraordinary structure known as Stonehenge from huge stones, some of which approach fifty tons in weight and twenty feet in height. Stonehenge also exhibits refinements which do not occur elsewhere in some of the other early stone formations. Using stone hammers, men squared and dressed the stones, made accurate joints and fittings, and shaped the lintel stones into curves to fit their own segment of the circle. It is believed that the upright stones were carved with projecting knobs that rested in corresponding sockets on the cross stones. In addition, the stones in the outer circle of lintels are fitted to each other with tongue-and-groove joints.

The construction of Stonehenge on the open plain of southern England is even more amazing because there was no local source for the stones used. Some stones referred to as bluestones were probably brought from South Wales, mainly by water on rafts or boats. The route most likely taken involved a distance of nearly 240 miles. Some speculate that the transporting of the eighty-odd great stones which came from Marlborough Downs to Stonehenge overland may well have occupied a thousand men for several years. With rollers and sledge, the journey to Stonehenge and back with a single stone might have

taken two weeks. At the site on Salisbury Plain the upright stones were probably tipped carefully into foundation pits and packed. The horizontal lintels may have been set in place by being raised on a type of growing tower made from timbers.

Controversy still surrounds the purpose of Stonehenge. Some believe the design is that of an astronomical observatory which served as a remarkably accurate form of calendar.*

Whatever Stonehenge may be, the massive stones stand for each of us to walk among and ponder their silent strength and mystery.

*Gardner *Art Through the Ages*, 7th ed., Harcourt, Brace, Jovanovich, Inc. New York, 1980

Cathedral

From vaulted depths the towers rise and soar
In pinnacles and spires that pierce the blue,
So men may glimpse, in Gothic tracery,
Their prayer ascending to the infinite.
With upward gaze the heart attuned beholds
Imponderables carved in quarried stone,
While stained-glass radiance pours sacrament
On faith proclaimed aloft in ringing chimes.
In reverence the builders here have wrought
An affirmation of the spirit's quest;
An aspiration rendered visible—
The mortal thirst for immortality.

David B. Steinman

I believe in God—
this is a fine, praiseworthy thing to say.
But to acknowledge God,
wherever and however he manifests himself,
that in truth is heavenly bliss on earth.

J. W. Von Goethe

THE CALENDAR

Without an organized calendar to count days, weeks, and years there would be no need for greeting cards. Without a calendar we could forget about bill paying at the end of the month because there would be no end of the month.

Alfred Cohen

1 Primitive people didn't use calendars. Their lives were timed by the light of day and the dark of night. For most of them there was no need to measure time because they spent most of it as nomadic hunters. These ancients, though, were aware that the moon's phases never changed and that between

2 one full moon and the next there were about twenty-nine suns. As their nomadic tendencies declined in favor of a more stable, agrarian society, primitive people, spurred by a need to forecast planting times, developed methods for charting time. The moon's phases were chosen as a measuring device, the

7 days before the Nile began to crest. This observation gave them time to warn farmers to seek high ground before the bloated river reached their land. Over a fifty-year period records showed 365 days elapsed between two risings of Sirius. Egyptians were a sophisticated, civilized people 5000 years

8 ago, and among the most worldly wise was a physician named Troth. He was sufficiently influential to have his ideas about construction of a formal calendar accepted by the Pharaoh. Troth used the solar years of 365 days to build his calendar. Since planting time took place toward the end of Septem-

9 ber, the autumn equinox, Troth started each new year on what we know as September 23. Each month in the year contained thirty days and was identified by the numbers one through twelve, as were the days. Seven-day weeks were to come much later. Twelve months of thirty days each ac-

14 ing some old ideas and introducing new ones in an effort to regulate time spans in an orderly manner. Before Julius Caesar put his imprint on it, the Roman calendar was a mess, riddled by arbitrary exclusions and additions. As leader of the invading Roman legions as well as

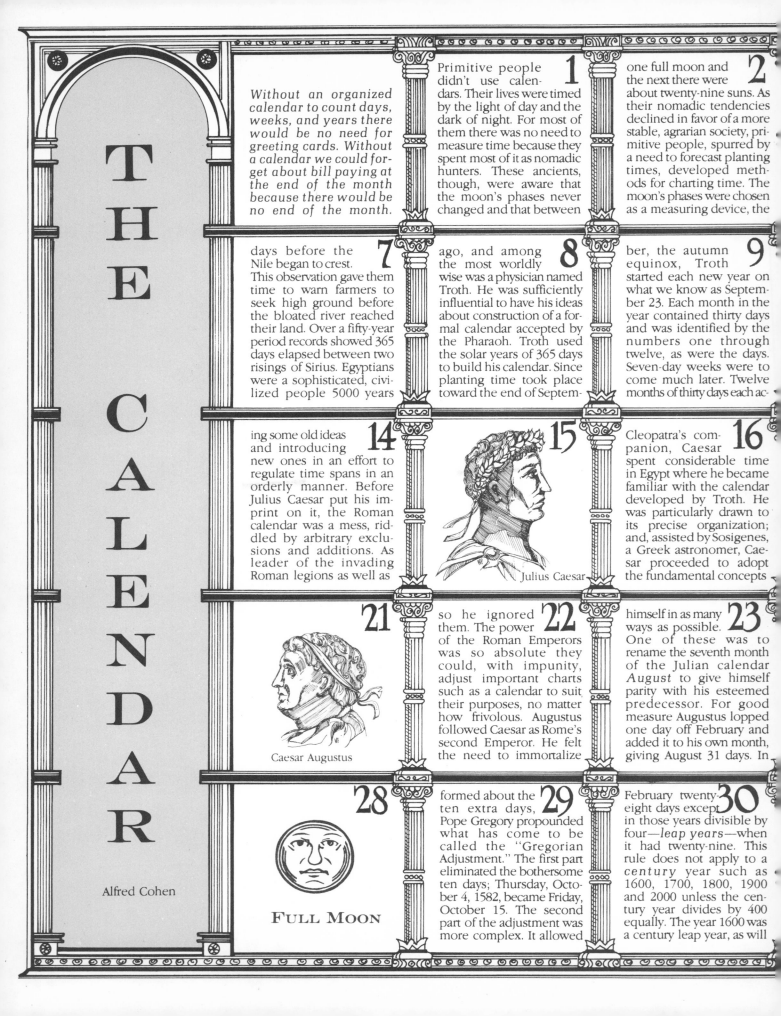

15

Julius Caesar

16 Cleopatra's companion, Caesar spent considerable time in Egypt where he became familiar with the calendar developed by Troth. He was particularly drawn to its precise organization; and, assisted by Sosigenes, a Greek astronomer, Caesar proceeded to adopt the fundamental concepts

21

Caesar Augustus

22 so he ignored them. The power of the Roman Emperors was so absolute they could, with impunity, adjust important charts such as a calendar to suit their purposes, no matter how frivolous. Augustus followed Caesar as Rome's second Emperor. He felt the need to immortalize

23 himself in as many ways as possible. One of these was to rename the seventh month of the Julian calendar *August* to give himself parity with his esteemed predecessor. For good measure Augustus lopped one day off February and added it to his own month, giving August 31 days. In

28

FULL MOON

29 formed about the ten extra days, Pope Gregory propounded what has come to be called the "Gregorian Adjustment." The first part eliminated the bothersome ten days; Thursday, October 4, 1582, became Friday, October 15. The second part of the adjustment was more complex. It allowed

30 February twenty-eight days except in those years divisible by four—*leap years*—when it had twenty-nine. This rule does not apply to a *century year* such as 1600, 1700, 1800, 1900 and 2000 unless the century year divides by 400 equally. The year 1600 was a century leap year, as will

3 time between the full moons named *moonths*, a word which eventually became *months*. Theirs was an extremely primitive calendar for a primitive people. Credit the Egyptians with developing the concept of the first organized calendar. Its origins were rooted in the Nile River which, fed by melting

4 snows from the lofty plateaus of Central Africa, overflowed its banks two months of the year. During this time the Nile became a huge lake. When its waters receded, enormous mud flats were left behind which, despite the intense heat, retained enough moisture for people to engage in

5

LAST QUARTER

6 farming ten months of the year. The Egyptians began their calendar to keep track of and anticipate the Nile's flood stages. Again, the heavens provided the means for calculating, this time in the regular appearance of the fixed star Sirius. Temple priests noted that this star rose in the sky just a few

10 counted for 360 days, leaving 5¼ days left over. Extra days were placed at the end of the year and, unlike ordinary numbered days, were given names of five dieties worshiped at the Temple of Osiris. The remaining one-fourth day was handled this way, too, when it became a full day every

11 four years. Troth also broke up his calendar into smaller time units. Thirty days were subdivided into three ten-day groups. These days in turn were split into ten hours, each of which comprised 100 minutes, one minute equaling 100 seconds. The Egyptians liked to keep things orderly. Of

12
NEW MOON

13 the men who succeeded in restructuring the calendar Julius Caesar, Pope Gregory XIII, and Moses were perhaps the most influential. Moses' contribution was limited to one area. It was he who first proposed splitting a week into seven equal days. The other leaders rearranged the whole calendar, adapt-

17 of Troth's calendar. The only major change he made was the way he handled the five or six extra days that cropped up at the end of the year. On the Julian calendar, as it came to be known, these extra days were tacked on the ends of alternate months. Although opinions differ

18 about how the months came to be named—Quintilus was renamed July in honor of Caesar—the arrangement of the Julian calendar resembles our current calendar in many respects. Put into use about 46 B.C., it accounted for 365¼ days, pretty much the time it takes for the earth to travel

19 its orbit around the sun. But "pretty much" wasn't enough. To be precise Caesar's calendar was eleven minutes longer than the solar year on which it was constructed. Caesar decided he wouldn't be around when those eleven minutes added up over a couple of centuries,

20
FIRST QUARTER

24 Caesar's chart the number of days in a week (they were numbered, not named) varied between seven and eight, the arrival of market days determining the interval between weeks. Three centuries later Emperor Constantine tidied up the Julian calendar by a decree which declared each week

25
Moses

26 was to be exactly seven days long, an idea he presumably picked up from Moses. By 1582, during the reign of Pope Gregory XIII, the minutes accumulated under Caesar's calendar had become ten days, presenting the pontiff with a dilemma he solved very neatly. When he was in-

27
Pope Gregory XIII

31 be 2000. Sometime after the year 3000 an extra day will appear during the twelve month time frame, but it is presumed that calendar makers of the time will know what to do with it.

The mere mention of Switzerland calls up images of the incomparable Alps and picturesque chalets, their balconies overflowing with red geraniums. However, my favorite memories center around one city—Lucerne, capital of the canton of that name. Pictures spring to mind of two bridges and the figure of a lion sculptured in rock.

At the beginning of this century Lucerne was a small, quiet town, ideally situated on the River Reuss, which flows into beautiful Lake Lucerne. But it has now grown into a bustling city of approximately 80,000. During the tourist season it doubles in size.

Famous landmarks in Lucerne are two remarkable covered wooden bridges: the Kapellbrucke

day's sightseeing was a visit to the Lion of Lucerne." The Lion may be seen in the Glacier Gardens toward the outskirts of the city along the main road to Zurich. The Gardens received their name from the fact that they are located on the site of a moraine that dates from the Ice Age.

During excavations in 1852, geologists uncovered a natural grotto in which the Lowendenkmal, the famous Lion of Lucerne monument, carved from rock, now stands.

The paw of the suffering lion, mortally wounded by the arrow in his back, lies protectingly across the coat of arms of the French royal family. The figure was carved in memory

Images of Switzerland:

Lucerne's Painted Bridges

(Chapel Bridge) and the Spreuerbrucke (Mill Bridge), built in the fourteenth and fifteenth centuries, respectively, and profusely decorated with paintings. The Spreuerbrucke is famous for its painting of the "Death Dance" done by Caspar Meglinger from 1626 to 1632, and the Kapellbrucke for its series of scenes from Lucerne's history, painted by H. Wegmann on the gables—the full length of the bridge. Nearby is an ancient water tower, constructed about 1300, said to have served as a prison and torture chamber.

Both bridges are fascinating to visit, but, quoting from my diary, "The high point of the

of the Swiss guards who fought to the death in an attempt to defend Louis XVI when the Revolution broke out in 1792. The king escaped, but he gave no orders to his guards, caught like mice in a trap in the Tuileries. Hundreds were killed.

The work for this moving sculpture was done by Lucas Ahorn from the design of the famous Danish sculptor, Bertel Thorvaldsen, in 1820.

Although Thorvaldsen's work may be seen in widely scattered cities of the world, including Warsaw, Munich, Stuttgart, Cambridge, and the Vatican in Rome, the design for the Lion of Lucerne stands as one of his greatest—surely a perfect symbol of supreme sacrifice for a cause.

Doris A. Paul

Woodland Cathedral

Patience Strong

Go into the woodlands if you seek for peace of mind — at this time when Nature's mood is gentle, quiet and kind . . . When soft winds fan the trembling leaves about the cloistered glade — and paths go winding deep into the green and breathless shade.

Where nothing breaks the silence of the warm and fragrant air — but snatches of sweet melody . . . and wings that rend and tear — the stillness of the windless dells where shallow brooklets flow — and shadows fleck the water as the sunbeams come and go.

An unseen Presence walks the woods . . . A sense of holy things — haunts the dim Cathedral aisles; and every bird that sings — is like some morning chorister, and every breath of air — seems to bring the secret murmur of a whispered prayer.

©

On these pages
we are presenting a selection
from Vacation Ideals 1956.

In the Forest

Patience Strong

In the forest we can rise
above our worldly care;
in the forest we may find
tranquillity, and share
— the silence and the
secret strength of great
and ancient trees —
sturdy oaks and silver
birches, laughing in the
breeze.

In the forest we can learn
life's lessons if we will;
how to turn towards
the sunshine, standing
straight and still — how
to be content with slow
development — and grow,
in grace and strength in
spite of storms, of wind
and frost and snow . . .
Countless birds and in-
sects seek protection in
the tree — food and
shelter; isn't this true
hospitality? And when
winds have stripped the
branches of their sum-
mer dress — they survive
to show the world new
forms of loveliness.

Stately tree! Look down
on me — and teach me
how to be — Strong and
wise — To live my days
in quiet dignity . . . In
the forest silences our
petty warfares cease. In
God's own cathedral
we discover Truth and
Peace.

The Isles of Greece

The isles of Greece! The isles of Greece!
 Where burning Sappho loved and sung,
Where grew the arts of war and peace,
 Where Delos rose and Phoebus sprung!
Eternal summer gilds them yet,
But all, except their sun, is set.

The Scian and the Teian muse,
 The hero's harp, the lover's lute,
Have found the fame your shores refuse;
 Their place of birth alone is mute
To sounds which echo further west
Than your sires' "Islands of the Blest."

Lord Byron

We have received several requests from our readers asking for back issues of Ideals. With that in mind, we have listed the back issues of Ideals which are currently available. We trust this will allow you the opportunity to complete your personal library or order as a gift for any occasion. Write: Ideals Publishing Corporation, Dept. 105, 11315 Watertown Plank Rd., Milwaukee, Wisconsin 53226. Include just $3.00 for each title ordered. Postage and mailing will be included in this price.

SPECIAL HOLIDAY ISSUES

Christmas Ideals '78
Easter Ideals '79
Mother's Day Ideals '79
Thanksgiving Ideals '79
Christmas Ideals '79

POPULAR FAVORITES

Friendship Ideals '79
Carefree Days Ideals '79
Homespun Ideals '79
Autumn Ideals '79

Special Issue!

Ideals proudly presents a timely patriotic issue, *The Spirit of America*. It's filled with 64 pages of brilliant color photography, capturing the panoramic beauty of our land. Also included are poetry and prose reflecting our nation's spirit, feature articles on historical sites which mark our early struggle for freedom, and profiles of outstanding leaders of our country. A foreword by Senator William Proxmire explains why Americans should be proud of their country and of each other.

Send only $2.95 plus 30¢ postage and handling. (Wisconsin residents add 4% sales tax on total amount of books ordered.) Your copy of *The Spirit of America* will be sent promptly. Don't miss this special issue!

ACKNOWLEDGMENTS

THE PONY EXPRESS by Samuel Clemens. Excerpt from *Roughing It* (Harper & Row Publishers, Inc.). AVOCADO-CRAB DIP; LOBSTER NEWBURG; SEAFOOD CASSEROLE; SLIMMER CRAB CAKES. From *Ideals Fish and Seafood Cookbook* by Patricia Hansen, Copyright © 1979 by Howard Hansen. REMEMBER PARIS? by Lorice Fiani Mulhern. From *Realms of Enchantment* by Lorice Fiani Mulhern. Copyright © 1970 by Lorice Fiani Mulhern. Published by Dorrance & Company. By Robert Louis Stevenson: FAREWELL TO THE FARM; THE GARDENER; THE HAY-LOFT; THE VAGABOND. From *A Child's Garden of Verses* by Robert Louis Stevenson (Charles Scribner's Sons 1917). Our sincere thanks to the following authors whose addresses we were unable to locate: Maude Ludington Cain for AN IRISH MILE; Dick Diespecker for portions from BETWEEN TWO FURIOUS OCEANS; David B. Steinman for CATHEDRAL.

COLOR ART AND PHOTO CREDITS
(in order of appearance)

Front cover, Photo Media; inside front and back covers, Houses of Parliament and Big Ben, London, England, Colour Library International (USA) Limited; Windmill near Dennisport, Cape Cod, Massachusetts, Fred Sieb; THE SPIRIT OF AMERICA, John Slobodnik; HOMOSASSA JUNGLE IN FLORIDA, Winslow Homer, Fogg Art Museum; THE LAND OF EVANGELINE, Joseph Rusling Meeker, St. Louis Art Museum; Sculptured Rocks, the "Sugar Bowl" of the Lower Wisconsin Dells on Wisconsin River, Ken Dequaine; Poppies on mountainside, Banff National Park, Canada, Freelance Photographers Guild; The Little Brown Church in the Vale, Nashua, Iowa, Tracy Sweet; Baldwin's Crossing at Oak Creek Canyon, Arizona, Fred Sieb; Double arch formation in Arches National Park, Utah, Alpha Photo Associates; Totem Pole in Big Room, Carlsbad Caverns National Park, New Mexico, Josef Muench; Mount Grinnell and Grinnell Lake, Glacier National Park, Montana, Ed Cooper; Waterbuck, Colour Library International (USA) Limited; Bald eagle, Alaska Peninsula, Rollie Ostermick; Volcanic splendor, Wizard Island in Crater Lake at Crater Lake National Park, Oregon, Ken Dequaine; Washington Sol Duc Falls, Olympic National Park, Ed Cooper; Hibiscus, Hawaii state flower, Ed Cooper; Hawaiian splendor, Chuck Gallozzi; Pont Alexandre III and Eiffel Tower, Paris, France, Colour Library International (USA) Limited; Rock of Cashel, Tipperary County, Ireland, Colour Library International (USA) Limited; Castle Neuschwanstein in foothills of Bavarian Alps, Germany, Josef Muench; Village church of Lauterbrunnen in Lauterbrunnen Valley, Switzerland, Josef Muench; Temple of Zeus, Athens, Greece, Josef Muench; back cover, H. Armstrong Roberts.